Vegetation Projections for Wind Cave National Park with Three Future Climate Scenarios

Final Report in Completion of Task Agreement J8W07100052

Natural Resource Technical Report NPS/WICA/NRTR—2013/681

David A. King[1], Dominique M. Bachelet[1,2], Amy J. Symstad[3]

[1]Oregon State University
Department of Biological and Ecological Engineering
116 Gilmore Hall
Corvallis, OR 97331

[2]Conservation Biology Institute
136 SW Washington Avenue, Suite 202
Corvallis, OR 97333

[3]U.S. Geological Survey
Northern Prairie Wildlife Research Center, Black Hills Station
Wind Cave National Park
26611 U.S. Highway 385
Hot Springs, SD 57747

January 2013

U.S. Department of the Interior
National Park Service
Natural Resource Stewardship and Science
Fort Collins, Colorado

The National Park Service, Natural Resource Stewardship and Science office in Fort Collins, Colorado, publishes a range of reports that address natural resource topics. These reports are of interest and applicability to a broad audience in the National Park Service and others in natural resource management, including scientists, conservation and environmental constituencies, and the public.

The Natural Resource Technical Report Series is used to disseminate results of scientific studies in the physical, biological, and social sciences for both the advancement of science and the achievement of the National Park Service mission. The series provides contributors with a forum for displaying comprehensive data that are often deleted from journals because of page limitations.

All manuscripts in the series receive the appropriate level of peer review to ensure that the information is scientifically credible, technically accurate, appropriately written for the intended audience, and designed and published in a professional manner.

This report received formal peer review by subject-matter experts who were not directly involved in the collection, analysis, or reporting of the data, and whose background and expertise put them on par technically and scientifically with the authors of the information. It was overseen by a peer review manager.

Views, statements, findings, conclusions, recommendations, and data in this report do not necessarily reflect views and policies of the National Park Service, U.S. Department of the Interior. Mention of trade names or commercial products does not constitute endorsement or recommendation for use by the U.S. Government.

This report is available from the Resource Management Division, Wind Cave National Park, and the Natural Resource Publications Management website (http://www.nature.nps.gov/publications/nrpm/).

Please cite this publication as:

King, D. A., D. M. Bachelet, and A. J. Symstad. 2013. Vegetation projections for Wind Cave National Park with three future climate scenarios: Final report in completion of Task Agreement J8W07100052. Natural Resource Technical Report NPS/WICA/NRTR—2013/681. National Park Service, Fort Collins, Colorado.

NPS 108/119713, January 2013

Contents

Contents

Contents

Figures

Tables

Executive Summary

A 2009 workshop piloted the use of scenario planning for NPS natural resource management planning in the face of climate change. Wind Cave National Park (WICA) served as a case study in this workshop. Available information and expert opinion were used to construct a set of plausible, future scenarios. Future strategies were then derived based on common themes that emerged from the scenarios. Workshop participants found the process extremely useful for fostering conversations about natural resource management in a changing climate, but they concluded that a more rigorous process for building and validating scenarios would make the resulting conclusions more robust to public scrutiny.

This document the application of such a process to WICA. Major uncertainties encountered when constructing scenarios for the 2009 workshop included how the direct effects of CO_2 on plants might mitigate warming effects, as well as whether park management practices would amplify or moderate climate-driven vegetation changes. MC1, a dynamic global vegetation model, incorporates these and other important processes (e.g., grazing) to simulate vegetation in future climates. We calibrated MC1 to the WICA landscape and then used this calibrated model to simulate vegetation in three future climate scenarios combined with a variety of fire and grazing scenarios chosen by WICA natural resource management staff.

Critical implications of these simulations are:

1. The current forest-grassland balance may be maintained, but at reduced tree biomass, with prescribed fires provided that targeted tree mortalities are attained. Moderate variation in the frequency and intensity of prescribed fires did not have large effects on these simulations. Prescribed fires have the potential to improve or maintain forest health, making it more resistant to mountain pine beetle outbreaks and wildfire, while preventing the incursion of trees into grasslands. Fire suppression would have the opposite effects.

2. The distribution of forest vs. grassland at WICA is quite sensitive to fire. Although no model can capture all the complexities that determine fire effects, increasing temperatures and concomitant drying of fuels are virtually certain. Simulations suggest an increase in frequency of high fire danger from 12 days per year in the 20th century to 20-100 days per year by 2100.

3. Future forage production was little impacted by grazing when up to 50% of aboveground production was removed, but prolonged 70% removal rates depressed productivity. Future annual forage production varied among climate scenarios, increasing in one and decreasing in another. Mid or late summer declines in plant production due to greater heat and drought could increase soil erosion and lead to late-season food shortages for grazers. Increased interannual variation in forage production supports the adoption of more conservative grazing regimes, particularly after 2030.

4. Given uncertainties in the rate of increase in greenhouse gases and the response of local climate to this forcing, long-term monitoring of production phenology, range quality, species composition, and, in wooded areas, tree density and growth and seedling establishment and survival is of great importance.

Acknowledgments

This work was completed with substantial input from the natural resource management staff at Wind Cave National Park and staff of the NPS Northern Great Plains Fire Ecology Program. We thank G. Schroeder, B. Burkhart, D. Roddy, B. Muenchau, K. Kovacs, and D. Swanson for their insights, guidance, and data. We also thank B. Keller and J. Millspaugh for sharing their range production data. This work was funded by the NPS Climate Change Response Program, with salary support for A. Symstad from the USGS Northern Prairie Wildlife Research Center.

List of Acronyms

AET	actual evapotranspiration
ANPP	annual aboveground net primary production
BUI	buildup index
Btu	British thermal units
C	carbon
cm	centimeter
DBH	diameter at breast height (breast height is 4.5 ft)
DGVM	dynamic global vegetation model
E_d	equilibrium moisture content under dry conditions
erc	energy release component
FACE	free aire CO_2 enrichment
FFMC	fine fuel moisture code
fli	fireline intensity
ft	foot
GCM	general circulation model (a.k.a. global climate model)
IPCC	Intergovernmental Panel on Climate Change
LAI	leaf area index
m	meter
min	minute
mm	millimeter
mo	month
mph	miles per hour
MW	megawatt
NPS	National Park Service
PET	potential evapotranspiration
ppm	parts per million
PRISM	Parameter-elevation Regressions on Independent Slopes Model
ros	rate of spread
s	second
VPD	vapor pressure deficit
WICA	Wind Cave National Park

Introduction

The effects of climate change on the natural resources protected by Parks will likely be substantial, but geographically variable, due to local variation in climate trajectories and differences among ecosystems in their vulnerability to climate change. The projections of general circulation models (GCMs) indicate the possible magnitude and direction of future climate change for a region, but the utility of these projections for more local scales, those of individual National Park Service (NPS) units, are more uncertain because the coarse-scale GCMs lack much of the topographic detail that alters local climates. In addition, complex, interacting effects of temperature, precipitation, atmospheric CO_2 concentrations, fire, and herbivores on the vegetation that is the foundational natural resource of many NPS units present challenges in assessing the effects of projected future climates on plant and animal assemblages managed by the NPS.

In spring 2009, Wind Cave National Park (WICA) served as a case study in a workshop assessing the use of scenario planning as a tool for park management planning in the face of rapidly changing climate. One outcome of the workshop was the recognized need for quantitative models to better understand the range of possible vegetation changes under different future climates and management decisions. This report addresses this need; it describes our adaptation of a dynamic global vegetation model (DGVM) to WICA vegetation and the resulting projections of future vegetation under three future climate scenarios and 11 management scenarios determined by Park natural resource managers.

Wind Cave National Park lies along a narrow transition zone between the ponderosa pine (*Pinus ponderosa*) forests of the Black Hills and the mixed grass prairie that once extended with few interruptions over the lower, gentler terrain, subject to warmer, drier climate to the east and south of the Park. The location and character of this transition is strongly influenced by fire frequency and intensity (Brown and Sieg 1999). Furthermore, the mixed grass prairie occupies a broader transition zone between eastern tallgrass prairie and the shortgrass prairie of the western Great Plains. The dominance of species characteristic of these two prairie types varies with soil moisture availability, evaporative demand, and recent grazing history (Cogan et al. 1999). In addition, Wind Cave lies near the midpoint of a long gradient of C_3 (cool season) grass dominance to the north and C_4 (warm season) grass dominance to the south.

The ecotonal position of WICA may make it particularly sensitive to climate change. For example, small changes in fire frequency and/or intensity and the vigor of trees vs. grass could dramatically shift the proportions of these two lifeforms. The Park hydrology is also sensitive to changes in the balance between infiltration of precipitation and evapotranspiration, as on average, only a small fraction of annual precipitation reaches the deeper soil layers that feed permanent streamflow. The resources at risk at Wind Cave NP include the Cave itself, as well as small backcountry caves, a genetically important bison herd, and other prairie species including the black-tailed prairie dog and endangered black-footed ferrets. All of these resources will be directly affected by climate change impacts on vegetation and hydrology.

Natural resource management challenges at WICA are substantial, diverse, and intertwined. Aboveground, the park has been recognized as exemplary for its high quality vegetation (Marriot et al. 1999), though the park is relatively small for the diversity of vegetation types and

1

species that it supports. Even without a changing climate, maintaining the integrity of the plant communities is complicated by the park's legislated responsibility to maintain viable populations of bison, elk and pronghorn. In addition, the federally endangered black-footed ferret was recently re-introduced to the park. This species requires large extents of prairie dog towns for prey and habitat. Prairie dogs impact vegetation by constant clipping, grazing and soil disturbance, thereby affecting plant composition and productivity. Moreover, naturally high interannual climate variability and the strong influence of precipitation on grass productivity in this region combine to yield high interannual variability in the amount of forage available for the wildlife that the park is tasked to maintain. Finally, fire, which is now primarily controlled by WICA and NPS Northern Great Plains fire management programs, is intertwined with all other natural resource issues at WICA, as it can impact prairie dog colony and forest expansion, ungulate foraging behavior, invasive plant species, and hydrological processes.

Although not capable of capturing all of these complexities, dynamic vegetation models do provide a means for quantitatively projecting vegetation futures in future climates under plausible fire and grazing regimes. Our work uses the DGVM MC1 to simulate the effects of future climate projections and management practices on the vegetation of WICA. MC1 is designed to project potential vegetation as influenced by natural processes and hence is appropriate for national parks, where conservation of native biota and ecosystems is of great importance.

Since the initial application of MC1 to a small portion of WICA (Bachelet et al. 2000), the model has been altered to improve model performance with the inclusion of dynamic fire. Applying this improved version to WICA required substantial recalibration, during which we have made a number of improvements to MC1 that will be incorporated as permanent changes. In this report we document these changes and our calibration procedure following a brief overview of the model. We compare the projections of current vegetation to the current state of the park and present projections of vegetation dynamics under future climates downscaled from three GCMs selected to represent the existing range in available GCM projections. In doing so, we examine the consequences of different management options regarding fire and grazing, major aspects of biotic management at Wind Cave.

Methods

Input Data

The MC1 model requires inputs of soil depth, texture and bulk density, monthly climate variables (precipitation, mean vapor pressure or dewpoint temperature, and mean daily maximum and minimum temperatures, averaged over each month) and yearly ambient CO_2. Historical climate data (1895-2008) were acquired from the PRISM group (Daly et al. 2008) at 30-arc second resolution (~670 m EW x ~930 m NS at the latitude of WICA). Soils data from Kern (1995; 2000) were downscaled to the same 30-arc second grid used for the climate data.

Future climate data were obtained from three GCMs chosen to represent the range of temperature changes driven by the IPCC SRES A2 greenhouse gas emission scenario: CSIRO Mk3 (Gordon 2002), Hadley CM3 (Johns et al. 2003) and MIROC 3.2 medres (Hasumi and Emori 2004). The GCM future projections were downscaled to the 30-arc second grid using statistical downscaling through the delta or anomaly method, as described by Rogers et al (2011). For each climate variable and each future month, anomalies between future and mean monthly historical (1971-2000) GCM-simulated values were calculated for each GCM grid cell over the conterminous US. Difference anomalies were used for temperature and ratios were used for precipitation and vapor pressure (capped at a maximum of value of five). Anomalies were then downscaled to the 30 arc-second grid using binomial interpolation and applied to the temporally averaged historical PRISM values at the same scale. Thus, a simple bias correction of the GCM-simulated mean recent historical climate is applied.

Model Description

MC1 is a dynamic global vegetation model (DGVM) that simulates vegetation distribution, biogeochemical cycling and wildfire in a highly interactive manner. The model always simulates competition between trees and grasses, where the latter term refers to all non-woody lifeforms, including forbs and sedges. It does not simulate individual species. MC1 projects the sizes of carbon pools in units of C mass per unit ground area ($g \bullet m^{-2}$), as is typical for DGVMs. Comprehensive documentation of MC1 and its mode of operation are given by Bachelet et al. (2001). Here we provide a brief overview of key components and their function.

MC1 has commonly been run at a resolution of 30-arc seconds to 0.5 degrees (Bachelet et al. 2003; Lenihan et al. 2003; Rogers et al. 2011). Each grid cell is simulated independently, with no cell to cell communication. However, drought conditions that trigger simulated fires are often region-wide, resulting in similar fire effects across contiguous cells. The model was formulated to simulate the potential vegetation that would occur without direct intervention by industrialized societies. However, the applications of MC1 have involved the indirect effects of humans on vegetation via increasing greenhouse gas concentrations, grazing and fire suppression (Bachelet et al. 2000; Rogers et al. 2011).

MC1 consists of three linked modules that simulate (1) plant biogeography, (2) biogeochemistry, i.e., carbon, nitrogen and water fluxes and pools, and (3) the occurrence, behavior and effects of fire. The model is run in four sequential phases: equilibrium, spinup, historical and future. The equilibrium phase initializes the vegetation type and equilibrates the carbon pools for fixed, vegetation-dependent fire return intervals and averaged monthly climate inputs. The spinup phase is run for a repeating loop of detrended historical climate data and allows for

3

readjustments of vegetation type and carbon pools in response to dynamic fire. The historical phase is run with historical climate data over the past 100+ years, followed by the future run, which uses downscaled future climate data from GCMs.

Biogeography module

The biogeography module simulates vegetation types and mixes of lifeforms. The module projects transient changes in biogeography through time, depending on temperature- and precipitation-based rules as well as biomass derived from the biogeochemical module. The lifeforms include evergreen needleleaf, deciduous needleleaf, evergreen broadleaf and deciduous broadleaf trees, as well as C_3 and C_4 grasses. Both tree and grass lifeforms are always projected together, though their relative dominance can vary as a function of climatic conditions. Lifeform mixtures together with tree and grass carbon pools projected by the biogeochemistry module determine the potential vegetation type from among 38 possibilities, 14 within the temperate zone.

In the transient modes (spinup, historical and future), the mixture of tree types (evergreen vs. deciduous needleleaf vs. broadleaf) is determined at each annual time step as a function of minimum temperature of the coldest month and growing season precipitation as smoothed by an "efolding" function. This function progressively diminishes the influence of each year's climate on the smoothed climate variables (see "Biogeography" below for details). Use of efolded climate variables reduces the flashiness of the projected tree types and was implemented to better represent the inertia of vegetation to short-term climate variability. The C_3/C_4 grass mixture is determined from the ratio of C_3/C_4 grass productivity, which depends on the temperature of the three consecutive warmest months, subject to the above efolding function. Higher warm season temperatures favor C_4 grasses. Pure tree vegetation types are projected for climate regimes empirically defined by thresholds of warm season precipitation and mean minimum temperature of the coldest month. Gradations from one vegetation type to another occur along the existing climate gradients.

The balance between trees and grass is determined by simulated competition between these two lifeforms, as mediated by fire. This balance is determined by the interacting biogeochemistry and fire modules, described below, and the resulting biomasses along with efolded climate are used in the biogeography model to define the vegetation type.

Biogeochemistry Module

The biogeochemistry model is a modified version of the CENTURY model (Metherell et al. 1993) that simulates the cycling of carbon and nitrogen among numerous ecosystem compartments, including plant parts and multiple classes of litter and soil organic matter. This module also simulates actual and potential evapotranspiration (AET and PET) and soil water content in multiple soil layers, the number of which depends on the total soil depth that is input to the model. Tree leaf and grass moisture contents are calculated as functions of the ratio of tree or grass available water to PET. These simulated live fuel moisture contents affect fire behavior, as simulated by the fire module.

Tree and grass production rates are based on maximum monthly rates that are interpolated from lifeform-dependent parameter values, depending on the mixture of tree and grass lifeforms set by the biogeography module. Maximum production rates are then multiplied by temperature-, water- and atmospheric CO_2-related scalars that differ for trees vs. grasses (Bachelet et al. 2001). In the case of trees, an additional scalar related to leaf area index (LAI, defined as one-sided leaf area per unit ground area), is employed. This scalar approximates the fraction of incoming light intercepted by trees. For grasses, scalars incorporating the effects of shading by trees and standing dead grass are also included. The temperature scalars are based on mean monthly surface soil temperature, as affected by canopy shading and reduction of outgoing long-wave radiation (Parton 1984). For WICA, the modeled soil temperatures are substantially higher than the corresponding mean monthly air temperatures when the vegetative cover is sparse and quite close to mean monthly air temperature under forest canopies.

Fire Module

The fire module simulates the occurrence, behavior and effects of fire and is designed to project large, severe fires that account for the bulk of observed fire impacts in the conterminous US (Lenihan et al. 1998; 2008). The module includes a set of mechanistic fire behavior and effects functions (Rothermel 1972; Peterson and Ryan 1986; van Wagner 1993) embedded in a structure that enables two-way interactions with the biogeochemistry and biogeography modules. Live and dead fuel loads in 1-hr, 10-hr, 100-hr and 1000-hr fuel classes are estimated from the carbon pool sizes produced by the biogeochemistry module. Allometric functions relate tree carbon pool sizes to height, crown base height and bark thickness for an average-sized tree. These are the required inputs for determining when crown fires occur and for projecting fire effects on vegetation.

Daily moisture contents of the different fuel classes and potential fire behavior are calculated each day based on pseudo-daily data generated from the monthly climate inputs. For temperature and relative humidity, a linear interpolation between monthly values is used to generate daily values. For precipitation, monthly values are divided by the number of precipitation events per month and resulting values are randomly assigned to days within each month. The number of precipitation events is estimated with a regression function derived from weather station data archived by the National Climate Data Center (WeatherDisc Associates 1995; Lenihan et al. 1998). Moisture contents of plant parts passed from the biogeochemistry module determine live fuel moisture contents. A combination of the Canadian Fine Fuel Moisture Code (Van Wagner and Pickett 1985) and the National Fire Danger Rating System (Bradshaw et al. 1983) is used to estimate dead fuel moisture contents.

Potential fire behavior (including rate of spread) is calculated each day based on daily-interpolated fuel loads, moisture contents and weather. Potential fire behavior is modulated by vegetation type, which affects fuel properties and realized wind speeds (higher for grasslands than forest). Actual fire is projected whenever the calculated rate of spread is greater than zero and user-specified thresholds are exceeded for the fine fuel moisture code (FFMC) and the buildup index (BUI) of the Canadian fire weather index system. These two indices are inverse functions of fine fuel and coarser fuel moisture contents, respectively, as specified by Van Wagner and Pickett (1985). Only one fire is simulated per year per cell on the first day when all thresholds are exceeded. Note that the day and year of fire may vary from cell to cell, given the independent simulation of each cell.

Calibration for Wind Cave National Park

Our goal in calibrating the model has been to approximate current vegetation distribution and ecosystem dynamics of the Park and to provide a realistic baseline for assessing the likely impacts of selected future climate scenarios. Meeting this goal has required a number of changes to parameters and functions within the model. Some of these changes are specific to Wind Cave and others will be incorporated into MC1 as general improvements to the model.

Substantial changes have been made in the simulation of tree LAI and fire. MC1 has typically been run over large regions that include tree species that develop dense canopies on moist fertile sites. Hence, the usual parameterization has included a high maximum LAI. However, within WICA, a single evergreen conifer (ponderosa pine) comprises nearly all of the tree biomass, with only small areas dominated by deciduous shrubs (Cogan et al. 1999). A few deciduous tree species are present, but too rare to be mapped as separate vegetation types (Cogan et al. 1999). Ponderosa pine stands cast less dense shade than do typical forests of wetter areas and MC1 was re-parameterized accordingly.

Before the advent of fire suppression, ponderosa pine forests were subject to less severe fire effects than those typically simulated by MC1 (Allen et al. 2002) and surface fires were common in the southern Black Hills in presettlement times (Brown and Sieg 1999). Therefore, we altered fuel loadings in the fire module such that simulated crown fires are rare in the more open mature forests that developed under presettlement fire frequencies in this area. This change makes it possible for MC1 to project ponderosa pine forest, instead of grassland, when fire ignition thresholds are adjusted to approximate presettlement fire frequencies for the southern Black Hills region. These and other changes are described below.

Water Balance

The biogeochemical module updates the soil water status each month by first calculating surface runoff (i.e. overland flow) as a fixed function of monthly precipitation. Surface evaporation (including water intercepted by foliage) and plant transpiration are then calculated as functions of potential evapotranspiration (PET), leaf biomass and distribution of water among the soil layers. Monthly streamflow is estimated as the sum of surface runoff, throughflow and a residual baseflow. However, the original formulation (Bachelet et al. 2001) overestimated streamflow, as compared to the gauged Beaver Creek watershed in and adjacent to WICA. We therefore reduced surface runoff by using the Century4 - VEMAP formulation, as documented in http://www.nrel.colostate.edu/projects/century5/reference/html/Century/submodel-wt.htm#water_budget. This formulation yields little bias in projected annual streamflows for USA watersheds, including one located in eastern South Dakota (Gordon et al. 2004). The updated runoff calculation sets surface runoff = 0 when monthly precipitation $\leq$ 8 cm and surface runoff = 0.15 x (precipitation – 8) for wetter months. This formulation substantially reduced projected streamflows for the WICA area and more nearly matched observed long-term gauged flows for the Beaver Creek Watershed.

Tree Production

The projected net primary production rate of trees is strongly influenced by the maximum production parameter PRDX(4) and to a lesser extent by MAXLAI, the asymptotic maximum LAI that is approached as live forest carbon becomes very high. We reduced MAXLAI from the usual value of 10 for all tree types to 5, given that LAI seldom exceeds 4 in ponderosa pine stands (Cannell 1982). We set PRDX(4) = 160 g C•m^{-2}•mo^{-1} to adjust tree production following the change in MAXLAI.

We also decreased the degree to which water deficits limit projected tree production by altering the water effects scalar, pptprd, which multiplies production by a value ranging from 1 for months of high precipitation or large stores of soil water to 0, when little or no water is available to trees. In our WICA version, pptrd = 1 when (monthly precipitation + soil water available to trees)/PET > 0.8 and is ramped down to 0 as this ratio declines to 0. This formulation replaces a function that ramps down to zero when the above ratio is 0.5 or larger (depending on soil texture), which may to be too water-sensitive for most trees. Mature ponderosa pines are deep-rooted and have been found to show little reduction in daily net primary production (NPP) under substantial soil moisture deficits (King et al. 2011).

The above parameterization results in an LAI of 3 - 4 and an aboveground live tree C of 7,500 - 9,000 g C•m^{-2} for old, unburned forests at WICA, as simulated with historical climate inputs. The latter range is higher than the value of 5,600 g C m^{-2} estimated from pre-burn plots in the area burned by the 2010 American Elk fire (WICA data supplied by A. Symstad), much of which had not been burned for more than a century[1]. However, several of the 29 plots lacked tree cover due to a recent wildfire and a few of the other plots had standing aboveground C values exceeding 8,000 g C m^{-2}.

Tree-grass Competition and Recovery from Fire
Another alteration of the model code affects the simulated competition between trees and grasses. Competition is ensured in MC1 by calculating grass NPP independently of grass LAI, so that grass growth is always projected under suitable environmental conditions, and by assuming a minimum effective LAI when computing tree NPP. This is achieved using the tree production scalar, laprod, which increases curvilinearly from a value of 0 for an LAI of 0 towards an asymptote of 1 as LAI increases to high values. In the standard mode of operation, if LAI < 0.2, a value of 0.2 is substituted for the actual LAI in calculating laprod. Thus, some tree production may be simulated even if tree leaf area approaches zero. This approach is reasonable for simulating regeneration following crown fires that are assumed to kill all trees – as regeneration from seeds or root sprouts may soon establish a new tree canopy under favorable climatic conditions. In this case local extinction of trees would be projected if their production potential were zero at an LAI of zero. However, this approach also simulates vigorous tree establishment in fire-maintained grasslands that are far from the nearest tree and may thus overestimate dispersal potential.

Our solution has been to greatly reduce the minimum value of LAI that is used in calculating laprod – to a value of 0.00001. We also reduced minimum values for carbon stocks elsewhere in the biogeochemistry module, which were included to prevent computational errors, so that this low minimum LAI is obtainable. This change projects a much sharper forest- or woodland-grassland boundary, as is commonly observed in the Black Hills region. To enable the

---

[1]Aboveground tree C calculated from plot tree diameter distributions based on allometric relations between tree height and diameter described in "Tree Allometry" and biomass equations for ponderosa pine in the Black Hills (Tinker et al. 1999).

regeneration of trees following crown fires, we lowered the crown fire mortality rate from 100% to 98%, which ensures adequate post-fire tree NPP to regenerate burned forests, unless the fire frequency is high. (See "Vegetation-dependent Wind Speed" below.)

Grass Production

In the usual mode of operation, the biogeochemical module of MC1 simulates grass NPP based on the maximum production parameter PRDX(1), which has typically been set equal to 300 and 400 g C$\cdot$m$^{-2}\cdot$mo^{-1}, for C$_3$ and C$_4$ grasses, respectively (Bachelet et al. 2001). However, we found that these values substantially over-predicted grassland productivity, as compared to (1) general production-precipitation relations for the Great Plains (Sala et al. 1988) and (2) transect-based estimates of forage production from data collected 2003-2008 by WICA park staff (unpublished data provided April 11, 2011). We therefore halved the PRDX(1) values to better fit these productivities.

A general relation between grassland annual aboveground net primary production (ANPP) and annual precipitation of Sala et al. (1988) projects about 2/3 of our average ANPP for WICA grasslands (with the above productivity adjustment). This relation is based on a long-term, comprehensive Soil Conservation Service data set that appears to have equated ANPP to that measured by clipping, presumably near the time of maximum standing biomass (USDA SCS 1976; Joyce et al. 1986). Thus, the simulated maximum aboveground live biomass for the no grazing case (which is about 3/4 of simulated ANPP) is a better match to the "ANPP" used by Sala et al. (1988).

Grazing

MC1 has multiple options for simulating grazing effects on grass production and belowground allocation. These options include both a linear decline in monthly production with increasing grazing removal fraction and a quadratic effect, in which light grazing stimulates production, but increasingly heavy grazing causes an increasingly steeper decline in production. Based on reviews of grazing impacts on rangelands (Milchunas and Lauenroth 1993; Holecheck et al 1999), we wrote a grazing algorithm that is intermediate between these two options. We assume no effect on production for grazing removal fractions between 0 and 0.3 per month and a quadratic decline to zero production as the removal fraction increases from 0.3 to 0.9 (Figure 1). We also assume a linear decline in belowground allocation with increasing grazing removal fraction.

This grazing algorithm is applied from April through September (i.e. throughout most of the growing season) during which 30% of live grass production and 3% of standing dead grass (10% of the live grass removal rate) are removed. These rates are consistent with MC1 grazing options included in the standard parameter files. For the rest of the year, we assumed a standard winter grazing effect with a production removal fraction of 0.07 and removal fraction of 0.15 applied to standing dead grass. We used these rates for all model runs except those investigating specific grazing management scenarios, which modified only the live grass consumption rate in the future (see "Management Options" below).

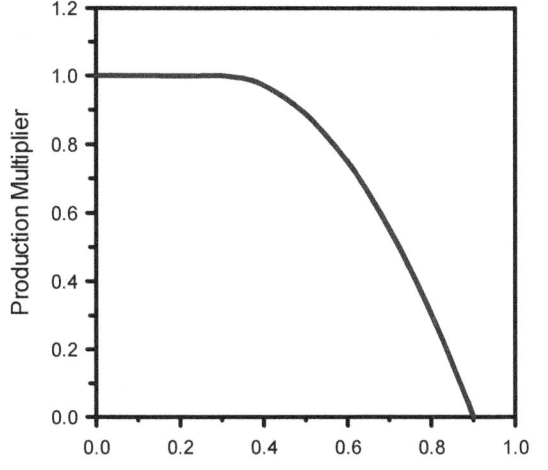

Figure 1. Grazing effect function.

The grazing effect scalar is a function of the fraction of monthly aboveground grass production removed by grazers.

Biogeography

The mix of simulated tree and grass lifeforms depends on climate inputs, which are smoothed with an efolding function to reduce the abruptness of changes in long-lived trees and typically perennial grasses. Each monthly precipitation and temperature value is smoothed with respect to the previous year's value for that month by calculating a running mean as follows:

$$y_t = y_{t-1}e^{-1/T} + x_t(1 - e^{-1/T}) \qquad (1)$$

where x_t and y_t are respectively, the unsmoothed and smoothed values for the current month, y_{t-1} is that month's smoothed value for the previous year and T is the smoothing parameter in years (Daly et al. 2000). This approach progressively reduces the effects of past years climate on the current year's smoothed value. For the usual T value of 10, equation (1) weights the previous year's smoothed value by a factor of 0.905 and the current month's unsmoothed value by a factor of 0.095.

The T value of 10 may be appropriate for estimating the mix of interdigitating C_3 and C_4 grasses, but it seems short for estimating the mix of longer-lived trees. We therefore increased T to 15 years, as a better compromise for the smoothing function. Use of this value for the simulation of current vegetation results in a projected tree type that is nearly pure evergreen needleleaf for the WICA area throughout the past century, as determined by limited warm season rainfall and moderately cold winters (mean minimum temperature of coldest month ≈-12° C).

However, for the wetter CSIRO future climate scenario (see Results, "Future Climate"), a large deciduous broadleaf component was at times projected for the tree type. Such a rapid change seems unreasonable, given the current rarity of seed sources for deciduous trees and the effects of browsers in preventing the establishment of new deciduous trees at WICA (Ripple and

Beschta 2007). Given the 50-year horizon of interest to park managers, we therefore chose to constrain the tree type at evergreen needleleaf for our future projections of vegetation.[2]

Tree Allometry

MC1 does not track the dimensions of individual trees. However, estimates of tree height, diameter at breast height (DBH), crown base height and bark thickness are required by the fire module to determine the occurrence of crown fires and calculate fire effects on trees. These estimates have been made in MC1 by first estimating tree density (number per unit ground area) based on Weller's (1989) relation between tree density and aboveground biomass per unit ground area for crowded stands undergoing self-thinning. Leaf area per tree is then calculated from this tree density plus the simulated leaf biomass per unit ground area. Tree dimensions are calculated from leaf area per tree based on allometric relations from the SILVA model (Kercher 1984) for *Pseudotsuga mensiesii* (used for evergreen needleleaf trees) and *Quercus kellogii* (used for deciduous broadleaf trees). However, tree stands may be sparser than assumed above when their biomass is low. Also, the allometry specified for *Q. kellogii* results in anomalously short deciduous broadleaf trees.

We therefore altered the allometric algorithm to calculate tree height directly from the simulated woody biomass based on the close relationships between log(tree height) and log(woody biomass per ground area) determined from Cannell's (1982) worldwide compendium of forest stand biomass and tree attributes. This approach yields greater similarity between the deciduous broadleaf and evergreen needleleaf tree allometries. For the WICA application we derived the following relationship from Cannell's data for temperate region pine forests:

$$tree\ height = 0.04071 * woody\ biomass^{0.628} \qquad (2)$$

where woody biomass is given in g•m^{-2} and tree height in m.

However, low biomass stands are typically more open and the LAI simulated by MC1 declines with decreasing stand biomass, implying the projection of a sparse canopy. That is, low biomass stands may often have lower density than those included in Cannell's compendium, due to the tendency of foresters to choose "fully stocked" stands for measurement. For such stands, the above equation would underestimate height because, for a given biomass, a low-density stand has fewer and therefore larger trees than a high-density stand of the same biomass. A simple, albeit rather arbitrary, way of addressing this problem is to assume that below a certain stand biomass, stand density is constant. As biomass per tree tends to scale with the cube of height for small trees (King 2011), this constant tree density implies that tree height is proportional to woody biomass$^{1/3}$. Thus, we assume that

$$tree\ height = 0.4689 * woody\ biomass^{1/3} \qquad (3)$$

---

[2] We also set the parameter "evergreen_selection1" equal to 4, rather than the usual value of 12 to prevent a switch to a deciduous or mixed deciduous lifeform when a precipitation value of less than 40 mm occurred for the summer month of minimum smoothed precipitation.

when woody biomass < 4000 g•m^{-2}, a value that is somewhat below the biomass at which woodland transitions to forest in MC1. (Here the coefficient of 0.4689 provides for a continuous transition in height between equations 2 and 3.) We also limited tree height to 27 m, as ponderosa pines seldom exceed this height in the central and southern Black Hills (Symstad and Bynum 2005). DBH is then calculated from height based on a diameter-height relation that we derived for ponderosa pine in the Black Hills from data of Symstad and Bynum (2005).

Following the calculation of tree height, crown length is calculated, based on the ratio of crown length to tree height. This ratio is specified for each vegetation type and tends to be greater for less forested vegetation types where trees have relatively long crowns due to less lateral shading by neighbors. However, the crown length ratio for evergreen needleleaf woodland of 0.4 specified in the standard MC1 version was lower than for evergreen needleleaf forest (0.5), so we increased the former to 0.6 for the WICA simulations. This change reduces the crown base height to 2/3 of its original value, increasing tree mortality and the likelihood of simulated crown fire for the evergreen needleleaf woodland vegetation type.

Bark thickness is calculated by multiplying DBH by a thickness ratio that depends on vegetation type. We altered these ratios for the WICA application by using the ratio of 0.063 for vegetation types with evergreen needleleaf trees, as is appropriate for ponderosa pine (Reinhardt and Crookston 2003). However, we subsequently used a fire mortality function for ponderosa pine that does not include bark thickness (see "Tree Mortality" below).

Fuel Partitioning
In the standard version of the fire module, the total dead fuel load is capped at 10,000 g•m^{-2} and then partitioned among the 1-hr, 10-hr, 100-hr and 1000-hr fuel classes by fractions specified by vegetation type. This approach is designed to link the loadings of standard fuel models (Anderson 1982) with the pool sizes simulated by the biogeochemistry module (Lenihan 1998) and to simulate severe fires. Using these fractions, 39% of the dead fuel load is allotted to 1-hr fuels in the temperate evergreen needleleaf vegetation type common at WICA, resulting in simulated loadings that are substantially higher than have been observed at WICA for this flashy-burning fuel class (WICA data provided by A. Symstad). These loadings also resulted in the simulation of repeated crown fires, which prevent the development of forests or woodlands during the model spinup phase.

We therefore changed the partitioning so that the different surface litter classes come directly from biomass pools simulated by the biogeochemistry module. This change was accomplished by assigning the large deadwood pool to the 1000-hr fuels, splitting the dead branch wood component equally between the 10-hr and 100-hr fuels and allotting standing dead grass plus a large fraction of the fine litter pool to the 1-hr fuel class. This fine-litter fraction was adjusted until the simulated fire effects yielded model output that approximated the current forest cover of the Park. For the final simulations, 86% of the fine surface litter pool was included in the 1-hr fuel class. As the biogeography module does not include an explicit duff pool and transfers material directly from the litter to the soil organic pools, this "litter" pool includes much of the duff layer as well.

Vegetation-dependent Wind Speed

A constant input wind speed of 3.5 m•s^{-1} (7.83 mph) has been used in recent applications of MC1, given the lack of comprehensive monthly wind data at the required spatial scales. Although lower than the reported mean value of 11.2 mph for Rapid City (40 mi NNE of WICA), we used this value for the WICA version of MC1, using other means to achieve fire effects reasonable for WICA. Actual wind speed at midflame height, the value used in fire effects calculations, varies from that reported at weather stations depending on vegetation structure and flame height. Midflame wind speed is generally less than that reported at a 20 ft height by fire weather stations (or at 10 m by National Weather Service stations) because wind speed increases with height above the ground and trees have sheltering effects (Andrews 2012). To correct for these effects, wind adjustment factors have been specified for a variety of fuel types (i.e., standard fuel models) or else calculated as continuous functions of fuel characteristics. MC1 uses the first approach, based on specified wind adjustment factors for each vegetation type. These factors range from 0.4 for most forest types to 0.6 for temperate grasslands, shrublands and woodlands, with a factor of 0.5 for temperate evergreen needleleaf forests. We lowered this factor to 0.4 for this forest type in order to reduce tree mortality and better simulate surface-only fires in forests.

Tree Mortality

MC1 calculates the probability of mortality due to fire in relation to the fraction of the crown killed by fire and bark thickness, based on a study of a variety of western conifers by Ryan and Reinhardt (1988). However, ponderosa pine is known to be fire resistant and likely shows a different fire mortality relation than the above. Hood et al. (2007) determined species-specific mortality functions, including one for ponderosa and jeffrey pine, which involves only the fraction of the crown killed (ck), as follows:

$$\% \ mortality = \frac{100}{1 - e^{2.7103 - 4.093ck^3}} \qquad (4)$$

We used this function for the WICA-specific version of MC1.

MC1 includes a minimum fire effect that is user-assigned, with a default value of 33% of aboveground C killed. The rationale for minimum mortalities in general is that MC1 calculates fire effects assuming homogeneous fuel and wind conditions across each cell and doesn't account for hot spots in an otherwise sub-lethal fire. For the WICA-specific MC1, we used an adjustable minimum crown kill fraction, which is translated to % mortality with the above mortality function. This method better links whole tree mortality and crown kill. For wildland fires, we set the minimum crown kill fraction at 0.10, which yields 6.26% mortality, based in part on our objective of simulating the observed proportion of wooded areas.

MC1 also includes a mortality threshold (typically 45% mortality) above which mortality is set to 100%. As we wished to emphasize burns with partial mortality to be consistent with the natural and prescribed fire regimes in the WICA area, we removed this threshold. We also reduced the mortality associated with crown fire from 100% to 98% (see "Tree-grass Competition and Recovery from Fire" above), to provide adequate leaf area for projecting post-fire regeneration without having to assume a set minimum LAI for this purpose.

Partial Burns

MC1 simulates a partial burn of a given grid cell when the time since the last fire is less than a vegetation type-dependent threshold. In this case, the fraction of the cell burned = (years since last fire)/(fire return threshold). The calculated mortalities and other simulated effects are then multiplied by this fraction, thereby reducing the fire effects. For forest vegetation types in the standard MC1, this fire return threshold is rather long (50 years for temperate evergreen needleleaf forest). In shifting the model to simulate more frequent surface fires, we reduced the fire return threshold to 10 years for the temperate evergreen needleaf forest and woodland and the temperate and subtropical shrubland vegetation types. The effect of this parameterization is to more or less cap fire effects on wooded vegetation types at a certain level as the fire return interval declines below 10 years.

Fire Suppression

A fire suppression algorithm was added to MC1 by Rogers et al. (2011), based on the rule of thumb that roughly 95% of fires in the western USA have been suppressed since the mid-20th century, but that the remaining escaped fires have accounted for ~95% of the area burned (Graham et al. 1999). Reported burn areas for WICA (NPS Northern Great Plains Fire Management Office data) fit the 95% rule remarkably well. Of the 101 natural fires from 1986 to 2010, the largest 5 accounted for 92% of the total burned area. Thus, high-intensity fires that have the potential to burn large areas are most likely to escape suppression.

The fire suppression algorithm suppresses fires based on thresholds for three fire intensity metrics: rate of spread (ros), fireline intensity (fli) and energy release component (erc). If both ros and fli are below their respective thresholds or if the erc is below its threshold, then the fire is suppressed. Rogers et al. (2011) set these thresholds at 100 ft•min^{-1} (0.51 m•s^{-1}) for ros, 900 Btu•ft^{-1}•s^{-1} (3.1 MW•m^{-1}) for fli and 60 Btu•ft^{-2}•s^{-1} (0.72 MW•m^{-2}) for erc.

We found that no historical unsuppressed fires and practically no future unsuppressed fires were simulated for Wind Cave with the above suppression thresholds. However, these thresholds were derived for the Pacific Northwest, where dense forests have high fuel loads. In addition, our changes in fuel partitioning (see "Fuel Partitioning" above) result in lower fine fuel loads than the version of MC1 used by Rogers et al. (2011). Reducing all thresholds to 45% of their original values allowed one fire on most of the forested cells at Wind Cave during an extremely hot and dry period in the1930s.

Controlled Burns

At Wind Cave, fire managers attempt to achieve desired mortality levels by conducting prescribed fires when weather conditions are safe and conducive to attaining these goals. However, the controlled burn routine in MC1 is designed to set fire on a specified day of the year after a specified number of years since the last fire has elapsed – so long as the calculated ros exceeds zero. For WICA simulations, ros does not exceed zero during winter or when the scheduled fire day by chance falls on a rain day. In this case MC1 attempts to simulate a fire on the scheduled fire day in all years thereafter until the ros threshold is met.

As it would be difficult to choose a fire day when the simulated fire effects met the mortality objectives, we instead specified the fractional mortality as a run-specific option. This was done by altering an existing option for setting minimum mortality effects to apply these effects to all fires. A limitation of our approach of using a prescribed mortality is that there may be a mismatch between this mortality and the simulated fire consumption of the various fuel classes. However, 90% of the 1-hr fuels are consumed in all simulated fires, which results in consumption of 77% of the fine litter, regardless of fire intensity, for our current parameterization of the fuel loadings. Typically, about 67% of the combined 10-hr and 100-hr dead fuels and 20% of the 1000-hr dead fuels are consumed on forested cells subject to controlled burns set in September.

Direct Effects of Atmospheric CO_2 on Plant Productivity and Transpiration

In addition to its action as a greenhouse gas, CO_2 has direct effects on plant physiology and growth. Under high light levels, photosynthesis is generally limited by the concentration of atmospheric CO_2 adjacent to the leaves. Plants exposed to elevated CO_2 generally show increased rates of photosynthesis, though this response may diminish with time, due to acclimation (Li et al. 1999). Over the years, other factors, such as nitrogen limitation of growth, may diminish the "fertilization" effect of CO_2, sometimes to zero (Norby and Zak 2011).

Elevated CO_2 may also reduce transpiration through its effect on the stomatal control of leaf gas exchange. Plants often, but not always, maintain a roughly constant ratio of internal to external CO_2 concentration, making the CO_2 gradient across the stomatal pores proportional to the external CO_2 level (Ehleringer and Cerling 1995; Gerhart et al. 2011). As long-term CO_2-mediated increases in photosynthesis are proportionately smaller than the associated increases in CO_2, this regulation results in a decline in stomatal conductance with increasing CO_2. That is, stomata partially close as atmospheric CO_2 increases, reducing water losses. Hence, transpiration is expected to decline with increasing CO_2, unless countered by an increase in canopy cover. However, leaf temperature increases as transpiration declines, due to diminished evaporative cooling – which increases the water vapor gradient across the stomata. The end result is a decrease in transpiration that is substantially less than that which would be expected were stand-level transpiration proportional to stomatal conductance. Nonetheless, there is pervasive evidence of reduced water use by crops, grasslands and forests exposed to elevated CO_2, particularly when expressed per unit leaf area (Norby and Zak 2011).

CO_2 effects are included in MC1 as scaling factors affecting production and transpiration. The scalars are logarithmic functions of CO_2 concentration, defined as

$$scalar = 1 + (co2param - 1) * \frac{\log(co2conc/350)}{\log(2)} \qquad (5)$$

where co2param is an input parameter (or the weighted average of parameters for grass and trees, in the case of the transpiration scalar) and co2con is the CO_2 concentration for the year of interest. Here co2param > 1 yields scalar values > 1, for CO_2 concentrations exceeding the reference value of 350 ppm and co2param < 1 yields scalar values < 1, for elevated CO_2. The latter case of co2param < 1 is applied to transpiration, as described below.

In past applications of MC1, these CO_2 effects parameters have been set to 1.25 for production (yielding a scalar value of 1.25 when CO_2 is doubled to 700 ppm) and 0.75 for transpiration (yielding a scalar value of 0.75 when CO_2 is doubled in this fashion). These values are supported by past reports of CO_2 enhancement of growth in open-top chamber and free air CO_2 enrichment (FACE) experiments on crops and young trees (Norby et al. 2005; Nösberger et al. 2006).

14

However, Norby et al. (2010) observed a gradual diminishment of CO_2 enhancement of NPP over an 11-year period in a *Liquidambar styraciflua* plantation and attributed this pattern to nitrogen limitation of growth. On the other hand, McCarthy et al. (2010) observed no decline in CO_2 enhancement of NPP over 9 years in a *Pinus taeda* plantation (both of the above plantations were 21-years old at last measurement).

Substantial CO_2 enhancement of sunlit photosynthesis of upper canopy leaves has been sustained over 8 years in 100-year old deciduous trees in a forest receiving high N-deposition (Bader et al. 2010). These trees showed an initial increase in basal area increment for the elevated-CO_2 trees vs. the controls during the first three years of the experiment, but not in the fourth year (Körner et al 2005). However, Sillett et al. (2010) found measurements at breast height to be poor indicators of wood volume growth in large, old trees and any CO_2-induced changes in the distribution of the annual diameter increment over the bole would not be detected by measures of basal area. Nonetheless, the current assessment is that no consistent significant increases in growth occurred over 8 years of exposure to elevated CO_2, despite substantive increases in photosynthesis, though the fate of this extra photosynthate was uncertain (Bader et al. 2010).

Results from multi-year FACE experiments on grasslands mostly indicate small effects of elevated CO_2 on photosynthesis and production when soil water deficits are small (Nösberger et al. 2006; Lee et al. 2011), but substantive increases in production when water is severely limiting (Morgan et al. 2011). In the latter study of a semi-arid grassland, evapotranspiration was substantially reduced by elevated CO_2, such that the combination of elevated CO_2 (600 vs. 385 ppm ambient) and increased temperature (1.5/3° C warmer canopy day/night) resulted in no treatment effect on soil water content.

Long-running experiments on trees also indicate lower water use under elevated CO_2 by stands with closed canopies (Warren et al. 2011) including the 100-year-old stand studied by Bader et al. (2010). Soule and Knapp (2006) inferred that historical increases in CO_2 have increased water use efficiency in ponderosa pines of the Pacific Northwest. Their inference was based on post- vs. pre-1950 increases in tree ring widths (controlling for Palmer drought index) that were greatest in drought years and for trees on dry sites.

Based on the above patterns, we see no reason to alter the parameterization of MC1 regarding CO_2 effects on transpiration, but have chosen to reduce the effect of doubling CO_2 on production from 1.25 to 1.15, for both trees and grass. The possibility that trees exposed to a gradual increase in CO_2 throughout life may respond differently than trees exposed to a step change as adults is an unavoidable uncertainty in modeling CO_2 effects, as is the fact that forest trees are of varied ages, depending in part on disturbance regime. A range of CO_2 effects on carbon allocation have been reported, with frequent increases in belowground allocation under elevated CO_2 (Jackson et al. 2009; Iversen 2010). However, we have chosen not to alter the current parameterization of no CO_2 effects on allocation.

CO_2 may also have less of an effect on C_4 than on C_3 grasses (Morgan et al. 2011), but we have not yet included this effect because MC1 currently applies the grass CO_2 production effects scalar to the combined productivity of all grasses (including forbs and sedges). Hence, the simulated C_3/C_4 ratio is affected only by temperature.

Simulation Protocol

We followed the standard procedure of running MC1 in an equilibrium phase, followed by a spinup phase with dynamic fire, a historical run and finally the chosen combinations of future climate and management options. The equilibrium phase was run iteratively with one year of monthly climate variables (monthly means for 1895-1950) for up to 3000 years to equilibrate the initial carbon pools. The spinup phase was run iteratively with a detrended 1895 – 2008 time series for a total of 1140 years to produce a quasi-equilibrium state in net biome production, as affected by weather- and vegetation-dependent fires. The historical simulations began in 1895 and the future simulations were run from 2001 to 2100.

Spinup and historical simulations were run with grazing implemented (30% of monthly grass aboveground NPP removed, April through September). The threshold values for the fine fuel moisture code (FFMC) and build up index (BUI) were set at 90.4 and 80, respectively. These values result in the projection of one to three fires over the historical period for most cells in the wooded northwestern part of the Park and 6 – 12+ historical fires per cell over the somewhat warmer and drier easternmost part of the Park.

Management Options

For each of the three future climate inputs we implemented the following options:

1. Natural fire with the same ignition criteria and grazing level (30% removal) as for the spinup and historical runs.

2. Controlled burns set at specified intervals (10, 15 or 20 years) with specified tree mortality (10, 20 or 30%) in wooded areas with the standard grazing level (30% removal): Although fire managers may burn grasslands more frequently than wooded areas (e.g. 8- vs. 15-year return times, respectively), we found that grassland cells were generally maintained as grassland in future simulations if burned at least once per 20-30 years. This, combined with the fact that there is no cell-to-cell interaction in MC1, makes the effects of a single fire over the whole park at a given time interval similar to the effects of fire rotating among portions of the park during that time interval, so long as the return interval is the same. Hence, for simplicity, controlled burns are simulated to occur throughout the entire park. These fire scenarios admittedly differ from the way WICA fire managers would implement fire management on the ground. For example, fire managers would aim for lower tree mortality as tree density decreased over time, whereas our parameterization keeps that mortality rate constant. However, MC1's capabilities are better suited to a general assessment of management effects than to a detailed simulation of a specific fire implementation plan. Thus, our goal is a general assessment of the effects of different management strategies and not the detailed results of particular plans that will depart from our idealized scenarios for a variety of reasons.

3. Fire suppression with only the more intense fires allowed to burn: Fire suppression thresholds were set at 45% of the levels used by Rogers et al. (2011), which yields one historical fire for most of the forested cells.

4. Three grazing scenarios with natural fire occurrence and 25%, 50% and 70% removal of herbage production in place of the standard grazing level (30% removal): The three

replacement levels were suggested by park managers. The highest grazing level is higher than the management target range, but it might occur due to complications in herd management, such as the inability to use certain population control options for a variety of reasons.

5. Projections with and without elevated CO_2 effects with natural fire and standard grazing level: An advantage of using a process model is that one can assess the contributions of different facets of global change to the projected changes.

Results

Historical Simulation

Important precursors to future simulations are the spinup and the historical (1895 - 2000) run, both of which set the initial carbon stocks for the future projections. When parameterizing MC1 for WICA, our aim was has been to approximate the current distribution of wooded and grassland areas, as well as the fire dynamics, at WICA during this historical period. The historical simulation in this section shows the degree to which we achieved this goal.

The distribution of wooded cells as simulated for the year 2000 shows an approximate inverse relationship to annual potential evapotranspiration (PET), which is in turn inversely related to elevation (Figure 2). The latter relation occurs because PET decreases with decreasing temperature and because temperature decreases with increasing elevation. As PET decreases, production becomes less water-limited. A slight increase in precipitation from the southeast to the northwest also increases projected productivity in the northwest part of the park. More importantly, the fire thresholds are exceeded substantially more often on the east side due to somewhat lower relative humidities there (also a correlate of higher PET). The importance of fire in MC1 is demonstrated by turning off fire during both the spinup and historical runs, which results in the simulation of forest throughout the park with only a minor difference in forest biomass between the more heavily wooded northwest area and the rest of the park.

The simulated distribution of wooded grid cells is in broad agreement with the current distribution, although with differences in details (Figure 2). Greater fine-scale agreement was attained for a northern subsection of the Park that was simulated at a resolution of 50 m using climate, soils and elevation from an earlier Wind Cave project that included slope effects on temperature (Bachelet et al 2000; Daly et al. 2000). We did not use this higher resolution approach due to lack of input soils and climate data at this scale for the whole park.

The high aboveground live wood biomass values simulated across much of the NW section may exceed actual values for this area of the park (see also "Tree Production" above). This difference likely reflects the long existence of simulated forest over the NW quadrant (including the second half of the 1140-year spinup run) and low simulated fire mortality in areas of high tree C. The simulated average tree height of ~18 m for the NW section is reasonable, given the observation of pines up to 28 m tall in a brief exploration of this area. The site index curves of Myers and van Deusen (1960) (used to assess site productivity) project heights ranging from 11 to 24 m for dominant trees of 100-year old ponderosa pine stands in the Black Hill region.

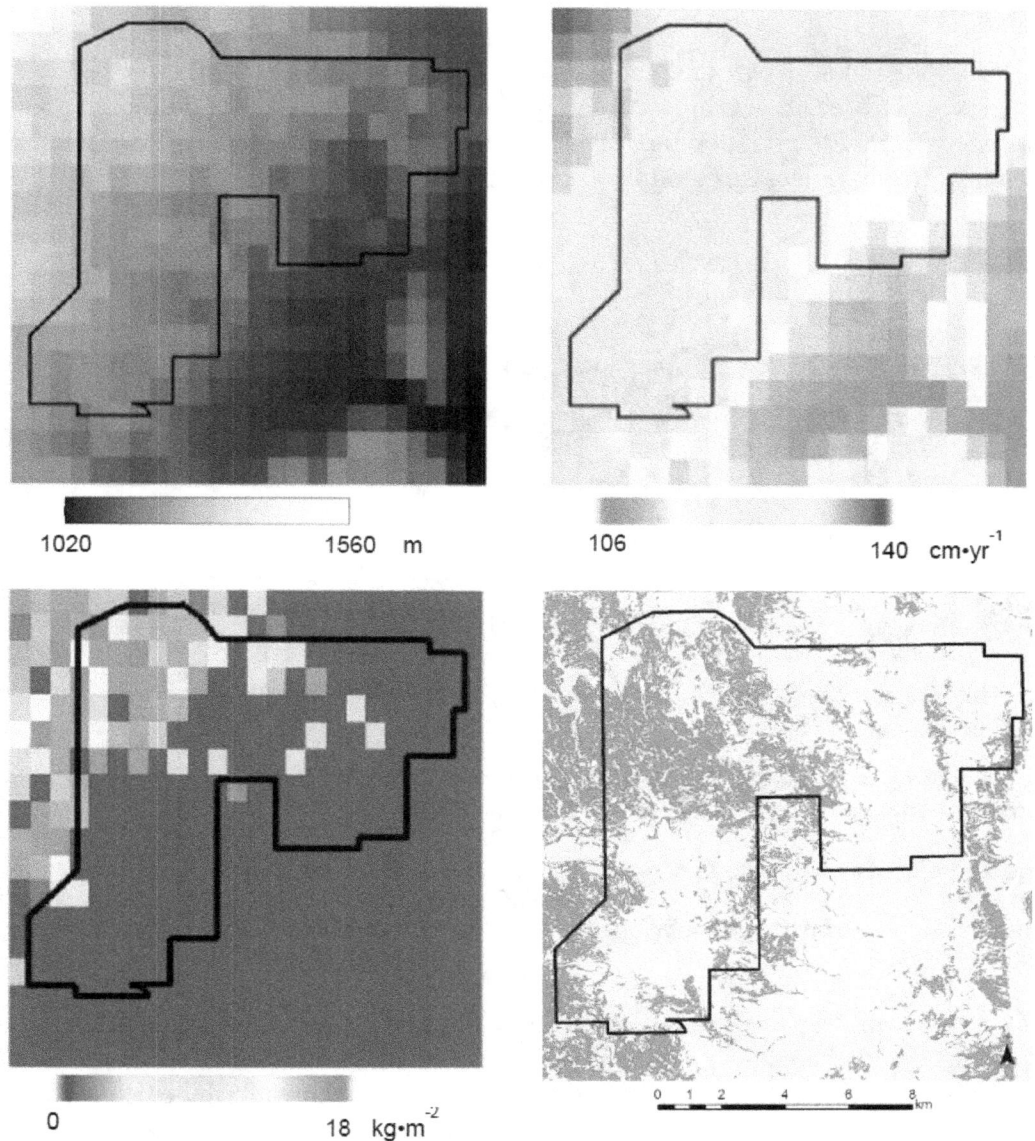

Figure 2. Distribution of simulated live aboveground tree biomass in 2000 (lower left panel) in relation to elevation (upper left panel), mean annual potential evapotranspiration (1976-2000, upper right panel) and observed vegetation (lower right panel; dark green = forest/woodland, light green = shrubland, tan = grassland).

Observed vegetation from Cogan et al. (1999): Dark green = forest or woodland, light green = shrubland, sand = grassland. Maps in this figure use the Mercator projection. Simulations by the dynamic vegetation model MC1 using PRISM climate data.

There are also distinct boundaries between grass and tree dominated cells, with strong dominance by one or the other of these two life forms over nearly all of the simulated grid cells. This inverse relationship is illustrated by the circled cells in Figure 3. In these, tree cover of moderately low biomass (3000-4500 g•m^{-2}, map on left) severely suppresses grass (20-56 g•m^{-2}, map on right). On the other hand, simulated fires remove tree seedlings and saplings from the grasslands. The yearly maximum aboveground grass biomass shown in Figure 3 is substantially lower for this default case of 30% grazing removal than for the no grazing case (data not shown).

However, grass annual aboveground net primary production (ANPP) is slightly higher for 30% grazing removal than for no grazing – probably because it results in slightly higher soil temperatures (affecting the temperature production scalar). Grazing also reduces standing dead grass, which somewhat increases simulated grass production.

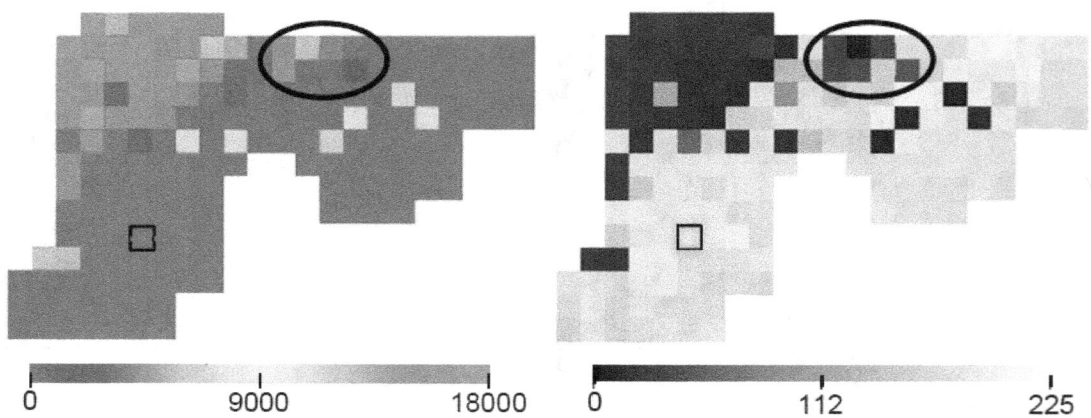

Figure 3. Maximum live aboveground tree biomass (left, g m^{-2} scale) and maximum live aboveground grass biomass (right, g m^{-2} scale] simulated for the year 2000.

(Equi-angular projection used here and in subsequent figures of the park.) The park headquarters cell referred to in subsequent figures is outlined in black. Circled areas illustrate suppression of grass by trees even for rather low tree biomass. Simulations by the dynamic global vegetation model MC1 using PRISM climate data.

The contrast between very low grass biomass under heavily forested areas and high grass biomass in non-wooded areas is in general agreement with the empirical forage production model of Keller and Millspaugh (2010), which was developed considering calculated estimates of forage production based on transect data collected over a period of five years. However, the Keller and Millspaugh model yields much greater variation in grass production over non-wooded areas than does MC1, which shows relatively uniform production across the grasslands in any given year (Figure 3). This difference reflects the finer scale landform classification used by Keller and Millspaugh (2010), which includes 18 range and woodland types defined in terms of soil properties and position on the catena between watercourses and ridges. The 800 m soils data input to MC1 includes only four different properties for WICA, and a single elevation per grid cell is the only topographic information that is input to the model. Thus, our simulations lack the subtleties of soils and topographic inputs required to estimate fine-scale variation in current forage production, but does include a mechanistic representation of the influence of changes in climate and fire regimes that are required to assess likely future climate effects on vegetation.

Simulated grass ANPP varied substantially from year to year (Figure 4) and was strongly correlated with annual precipitation (r = 0.75). Keller and Millspaugh (2010) found that annual forage production was strongly correlated with spring (April – June) precipitation during the current and previous year, consistent with the results of Smart et al. (2007) for a research station 140 km northeast of WICA. Our simulated grass ANPP was also correlated with current year spring precipitation (r = 0.50), but not with previous year spring precipitation. Maximum aboveground grass biomass per year was on average scarcely half of grass ANPP (Figure 4) due to the removal of 30% of ANPP by grazers and because some grass senesces before peak biomass.

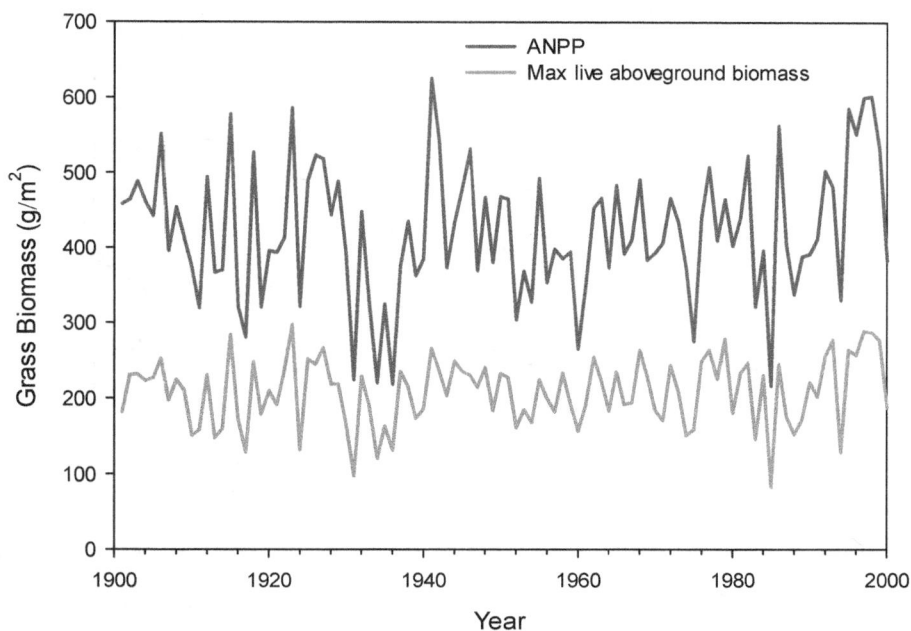

Figure 4. Simulated grass ANPP and maximum live aboveground biomass for each year of the historical run for the park headquarters grid cell.

See Figure 3 for the location of this cell. Mean historical ANPP of this cell is within 1% of the mean taken over all grassland cells. Simulations by the dynamic global vegetation model MC1 using PRISM climate data.

For the whole park, the simulated maximum aboveground grass biomass is slightly higher than the forage production estimated from transect-based biomass measurements done at WICA in 2004 – 2008 (Figure 5). Our model simulations of grass ANPP are about twice as high as the simulated maximum standing live grass biomass because the model assumes 30% of growing season ANPP is removed by grazers, as well as substantial grass senescence. Thus, the simulations of maximum aboveground grass biomass match the estimated forage production much more closely than do the ANPP simulations. This discrepancy may reflect underestimates of forage production from the observed data (a single late-season harvest may miss early-season or post-harvest growth, or calculations may underestimate total consumption by herbivores, including insects and rodents) or overestimates of ANPP in our simulations (they do not account for lower productivity in early seral areas or fine-scale soil heterogeneity). These differences reflect our calibration to the ANPP patterns of Sala et al. (1988), which were derived from sites of excellent condition (Joyce et al. 1986). Thus, our simulations could be characterized as applying to "nice" rather than real grasslands. Nonetheless, the current parameterization of MC1 appears to be adequate for capturing the year-to-year variation in whole-park forage production for a fixed grazing regime (Figure 5).

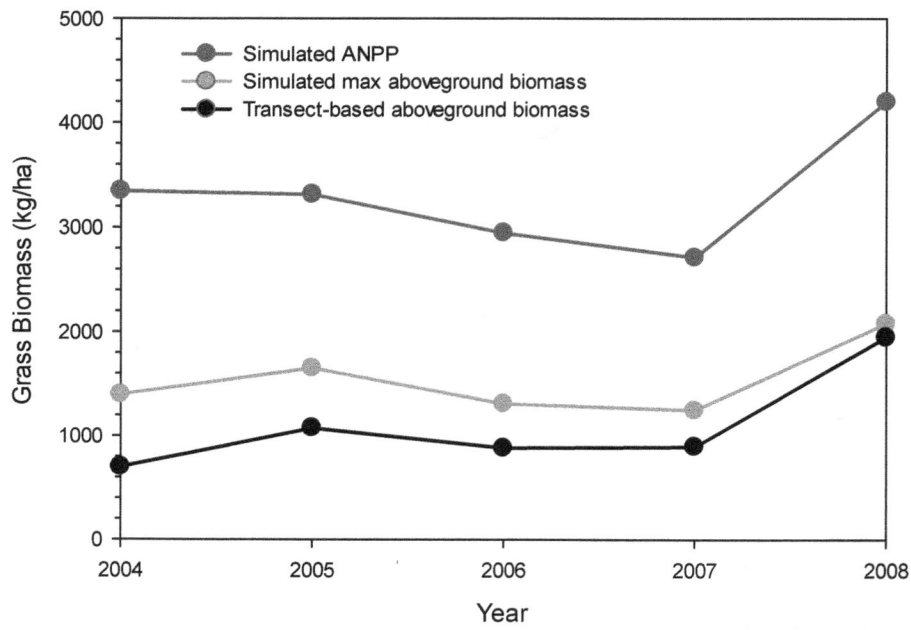

Figure 5. Simulated vs. calculated whole-park grass attributes.

Transect-based aboveground biomass values (black) are whole-park mean values for annual forage production estimated from late summer clipping measurements by park personnel, as given in Table 11 of Keller and Millspaugh (2010)[3]. Simulated maximum aboveground grass biomass (red) is biomass in the month of highest biomass for each cell averaged across all cells. Simulated ANPP (blue) is mean annual aboveground net primary production of grasses projected by MC1.

Future Simulations

The future projections are based on climate data downscaled from the CSIRO Mk3, Hadley CM3 and MIROC 3.2 medres general circulation models under the A2 anthropogenic emission scenario (see "Input Data" above) and are henceforth referred to simply as CSIRO, Hadley and MIROC.

Future Climate

For the interval of overlap between observed and predicted future climate (2001-2008), the future climate scenarios for WICA are relatively similar to the observed climate modeled by PRISM, with the most pronounced difference being somewhat greater and more variable precipitation projected by CSIRO (Figure 6). CSIRO is also cooler than each of the other three

---

[3] Keller and Millspaugh (2010) weighted the values for each site type by the corresponding area of that site type. For each year, the resulting mean was within 10% of the mean that we determined from the unweighted data provided by park personnel.

projections – by 0.6-1.3° C for Tmax, as averaged over the eight year interval. These comparisons are made for the park headquarters cell, which is quite close to the park-wide mean climate (0.055° C cooler and 1% greater annual precipitation) calculated from historical PRISM climate.

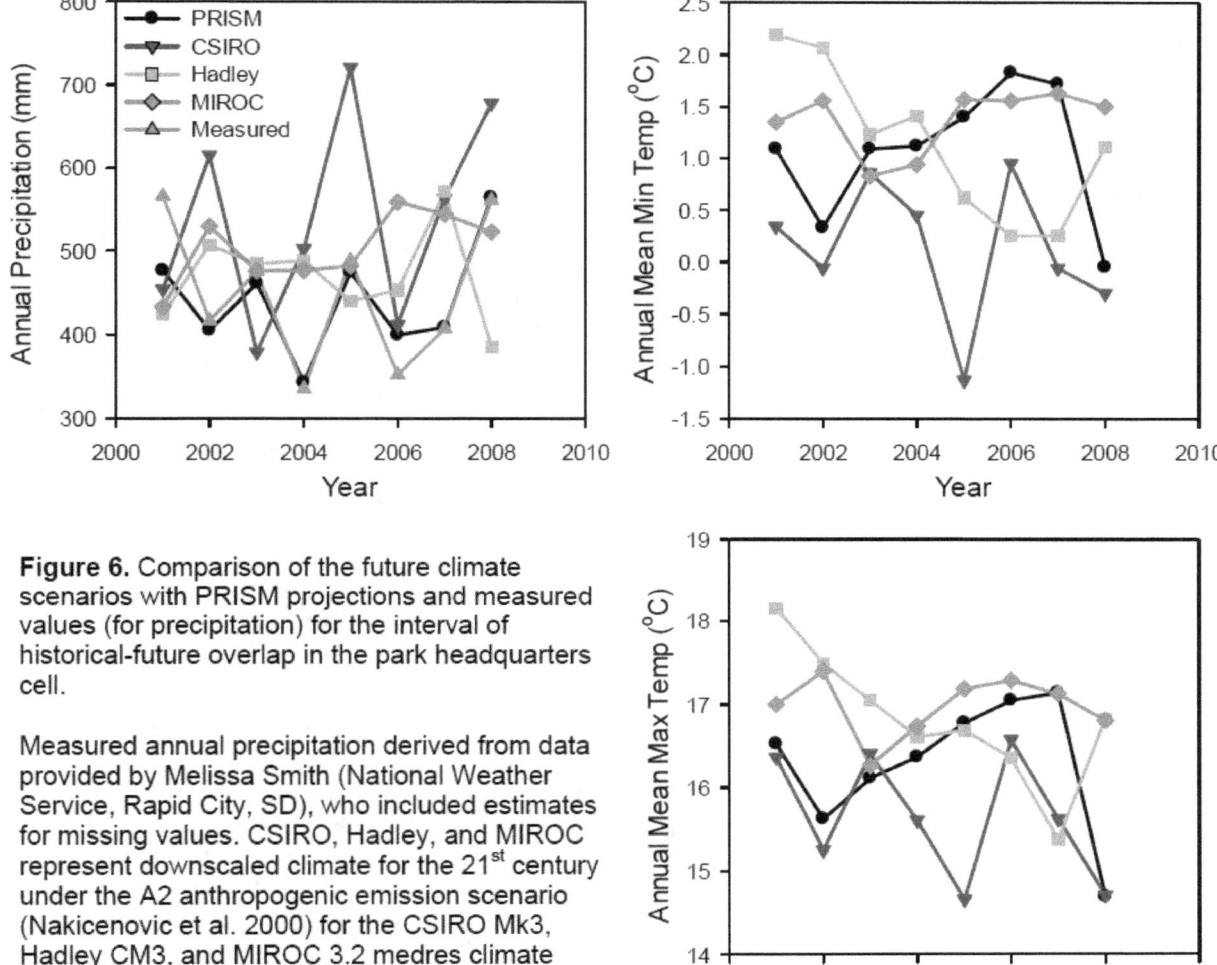

Figure 6. Comparison of the future climate scenarios with PRISM projections and measured values (for precipitation) for the interval of historical-future overlap in the park headquarters cell.

Measured annual precipitation derived from data provided by Melissa Smith (National Weather Service, Rapid City, SD), who included estimates for missing values. CSIRO, Hadley, and MIROC represent downscaled climate for the 21st century under the A2 anthropogenic emission scenario (Nakicenovic et al. 2000) for the CSIRO Mk3, Hadley CM3, and MIROC 3.2 medres climate projections, respectively (IPCC 2007).

Over the full 21st century, the three future scenarios show marked increases in temperature and divergences in precipitation (Figure 7). CSIRO is wetter and warmer than the present, Hadley becomes hot, but remains similar in annual precipitation and MIROC is hotter and drier than the present. These differences become increasingly evident in the second half of the 21st century. Vapor pressure deficit increases for all three scenarios, especially for Hadley and MIROC, due in the latter cases to large increases in temperature and modest declines in relative humidity (Figure 7).

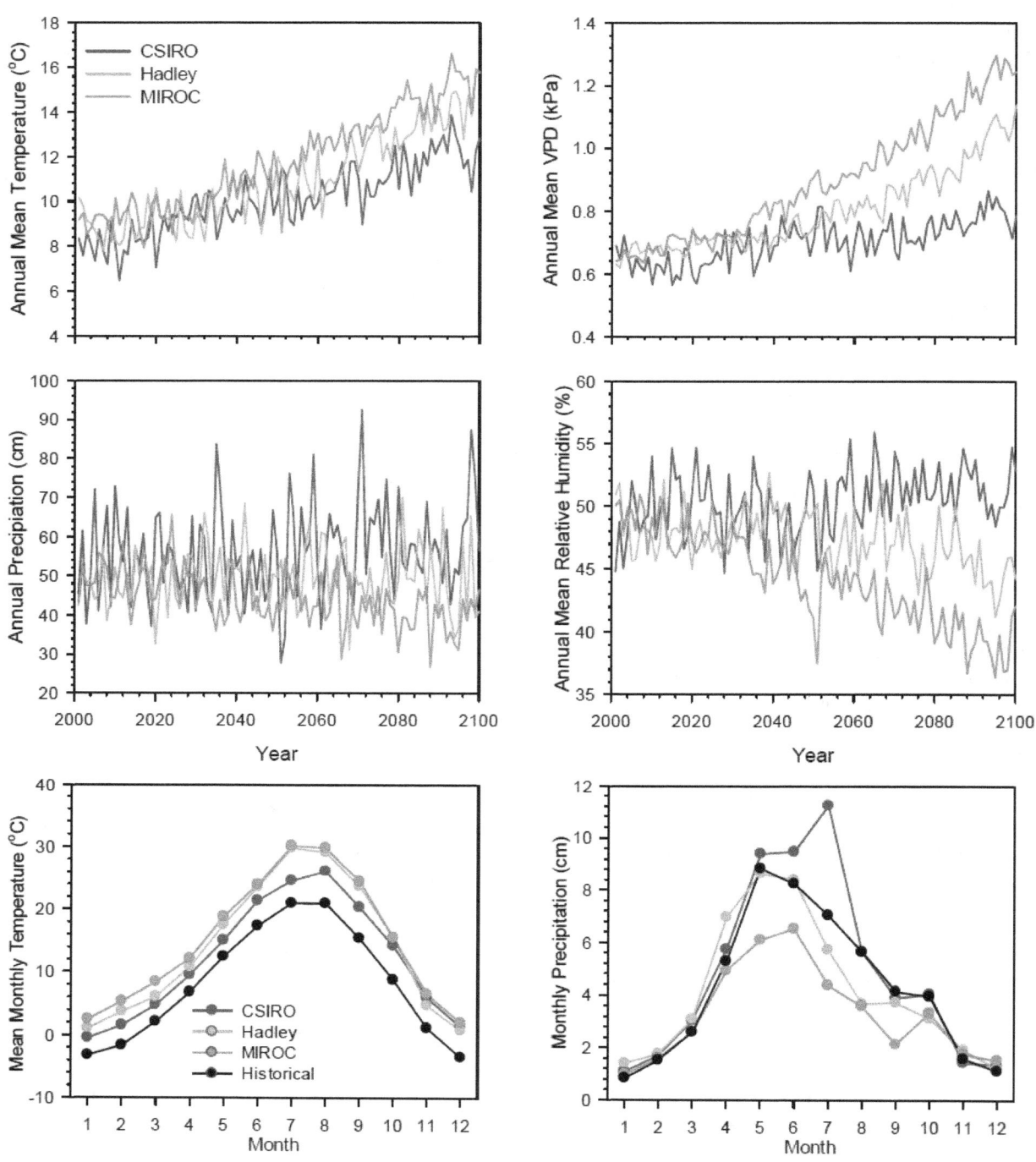

Figure 7. Projected climate at Wind Cave park headquarters for the three future climate scenarios.

Top two rows, annual values throughout the 21st century. Bottom row, mean monthly climate values for 2081-2100 (future climates) vs. 1981-2000 (historical). CSIRO, Hadley, and MIROC represent downscaled climate for the 21st century under the A2 anthropogenic emission scenario (Nakicenovic et al. 2000) for the CSIRO Mk3, Hadley CM3, and MIROC 3.2 medres climate projections, respectively (IPCC 2007). Historical represents PRISM values. VPD = vapor pressure deficit.

Future Vegetation with Natural Fire

The simulated frequency of natural fires is much greater for all three future climates, especially for Hadley and MIROC during the second half of the 21st century, as shown in Figure 8. This increase in fire frequency is associated with projected increases in temperature, and in the case of Hadley and MIROC, decreases in relative humidity as well (Figure 7). The likely cause of this association is a decline in fuel moisture content. The fine fuel moisture code (FFMC) and build up index (BUI) that are used to set fires in MC1 are driven by the equilibrium moisture content under dry conditions (E_d). E_d declines with increasing temperature and decreasing humidity – as calculated by Van Wagner and Pickett (1985). Under warm, dry conditions (~30° C and 40% relative humidity) an increase in temperature of one degree C has roughly the same effect on E_d as a 1% decrease in humidity. Consequently, under future conditions E_d decreases and the fire ignition thresholds are breached progressively more often.

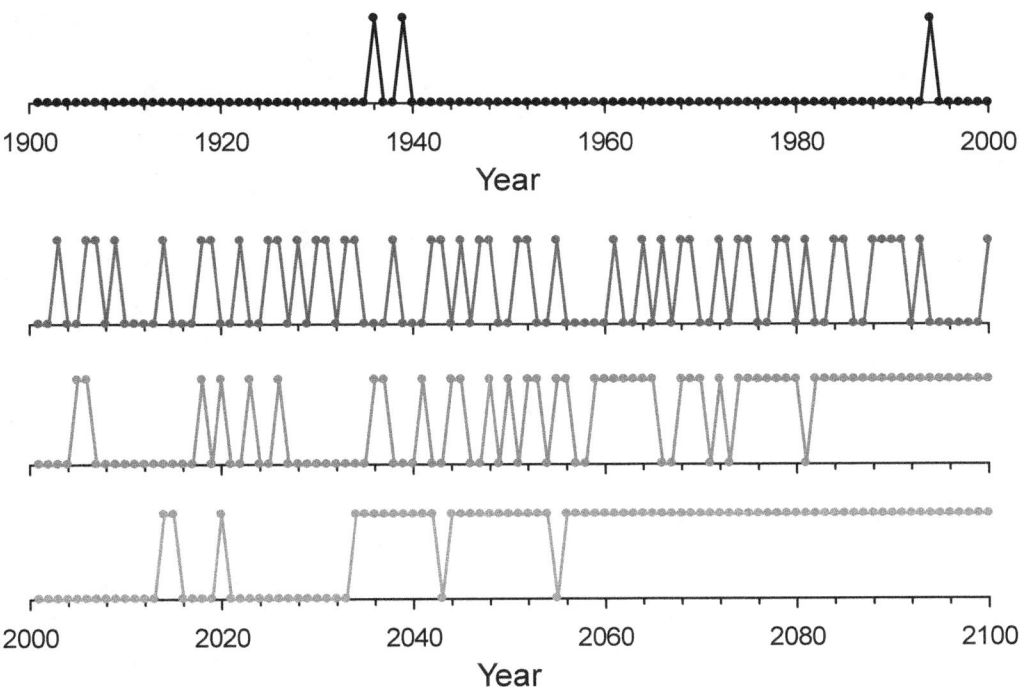

Figure 8. Years of simulated fire for a forested cell in the 20th century (top panel) and 21st century for the three climate scenarios (bottom three panels).

CSIRO (blue), Hadley (green), and MIROC (red) climates are those shown in Figure 7.

The above increase in fire frequency causes a reduction in projected forest biomass that is quite apparent by the end of the 21st century, particularly for CSIRO (Figure 9). In all climate scenarios, the fire return interval is less than 10 years, so forested cells are only partially burned in the simulations (see "Partial Burns" above). The resulting effective 10-year fire return time lowers fuel loads somewhat, limiting the effects of these frequent fires. However, the warm, wet CSIRO climate increases productivity, yielding higher fuel loads and therefore higher tree mortality in each fire. In all cases, the distribution of wooded cells remains the same and the initial variation in forest biomass among the wooded cells is somewhat reduced by the end of the 21st century. The latter pattern occurs because the cells with low forest biomass regrow more quickly after partial biomass removal by fire than do the cells with high biomass that are close to their carrying capacity, where losses due to natural mortality equal growth of the remaining trees. Thus, cells with low initial biomass tend to retain that biomass, despite disturbance, whereas cells with high initial biomass lose a substantial fraction of their biomass.

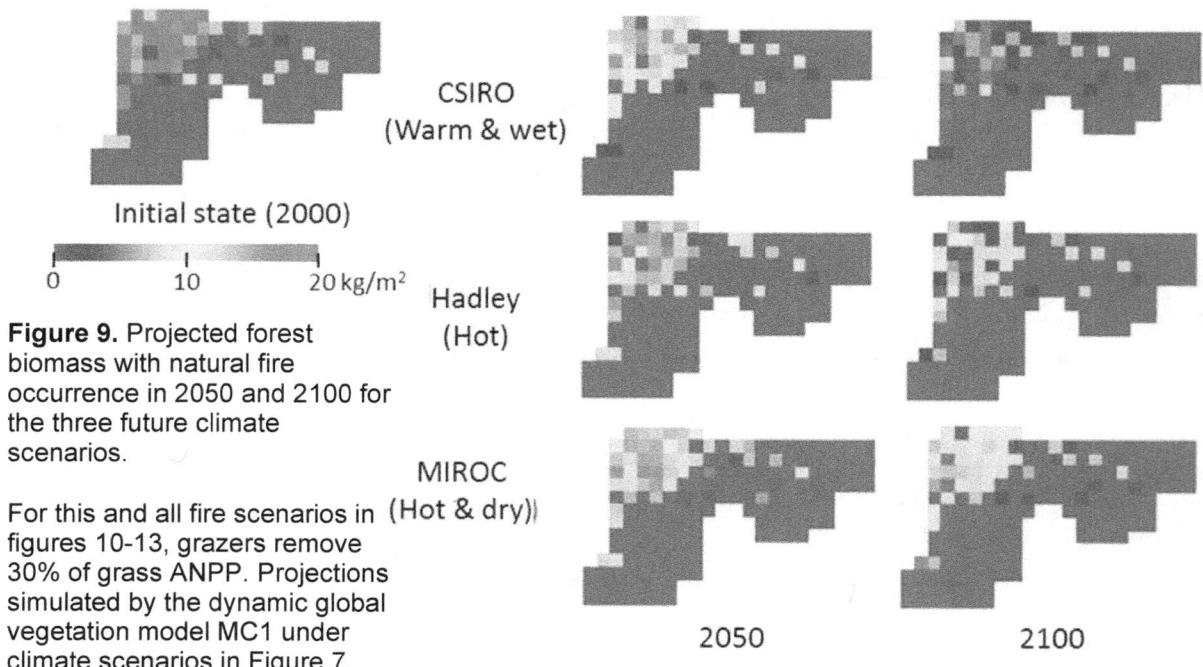

CSIRO (Warm & wet)

Initial state (2000)

0   10   20 kg/m²   **Hadley (Hot)**

Figure 9. Projected forest biomass with natural fire occurrence in 2050 and 2100 for the three future climate scenarios.

MIROC (Hot & dry)

For this and all fire scenarios in figures 10-13, grazers remove 30% of grass ANPP. Projections simulated by the dynamic global vegetation model MC1 under climate scenarios in Figure 7.

2050   2100

Fire suppression

The effects of fire suppression are illustrated in Figure 10 for the case where suppression is initiated in 1941, the approximate onset of widespread and efficient fire suppression in the US (Rogers et al. 2011). A more heterogeneous distribution of forest and woodlands results for several reasons. First, the suppression of fires for 60 years during the historical period produces a simulated buildup of tree biomass in the grasslands that is visually evident for a scattering of cells by year 2000 (compare the initial states of Figures 9 and 10). Second, future fires that escape suppression are of greater severity and hence result in greater mortality per fire than do the more frequent projected natural fires. Third, because small differences in potential fire intensity determine which cells escape fire, a patchwork of fire effects results. As grassland fires rarely exceed the suppression threshold, a variable incursion by trees is projected into grassland areas, depending in part on their initial (albeit low) tree biomass.

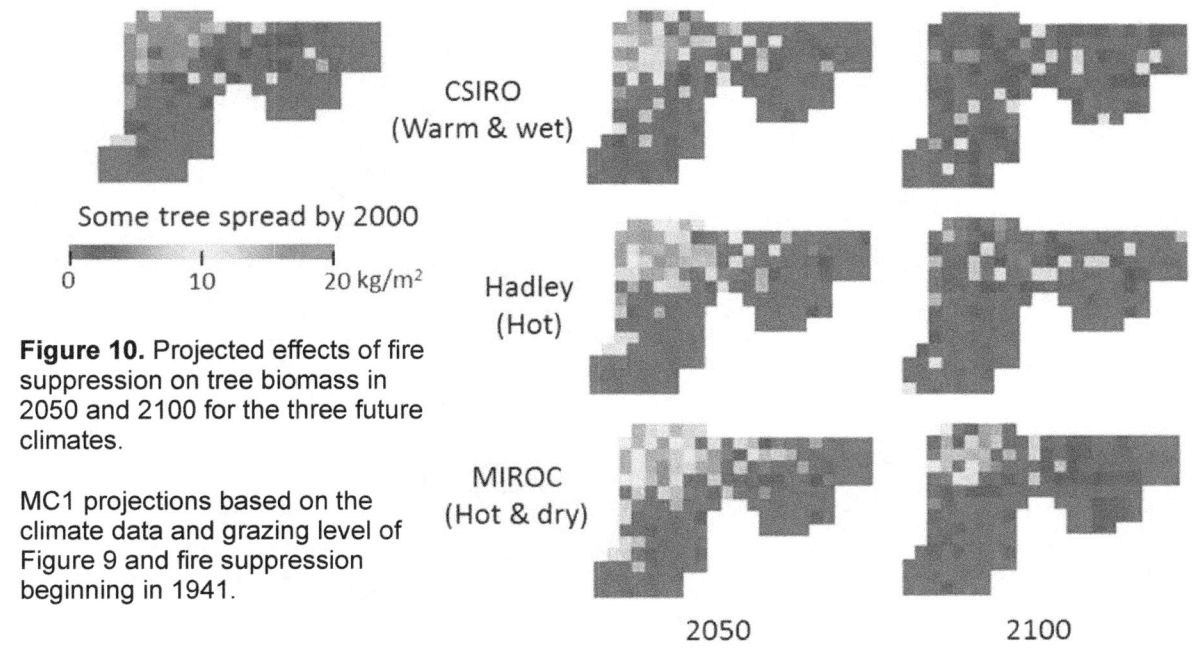

Some tree spread by 2000

0   10   20 kg/m²

Figure 10. Projected effects of fire suppression on tree biomass in 2050 and 2100 for the three future climates.

MC1 projections based on the climate data and grazing level of Figure 9 and fire suppression beginning in 1941.

CSIRO
(Warm & wet)

Hadley
(Hot)

MIROC
(Hot & dry)

2050   2100

Prescribed fire effects

The projected effects of regularly prescribed fires are illustrated in Figures 11, 12 and 13, based on the assumption of complete suppression of natural fires and complete control of fire effects by managers. Here, tree biomass is substantially reduced in cells with high forest biomass, but less so for those with low biomass, resulting in a more homogeneous distribution of projected biomass over the wooded cells. As was the case for natural fires, cells with low tree biomass recover more quickly from a given percentage biomass loss than do cells with initially high biomass. Wooded cells remain wooded and grassland cells remain grassland for the range of simulations shown here. However, the prediction of homogenous forest biomass is unlikely to occur in actuality, due to uncontrollable variation in fire severity and variation in forest productivity in relation to fine-scale topographic features not included in our assessment. Nonetheless, our results suggest that moderate variation in the timing and intensity of prescribed fires would not severely affect wooded areas, so long as extensive crown fires were avoided. Given that the initial tree biomass on the heavily forested cells was higher than typical for wooded areas at WICA, these simulations suggest that prescribed fires have the potential to improve or maintain forest health, while preventing the incursion of trees into grasslands, in all of the climate scenarios used here.

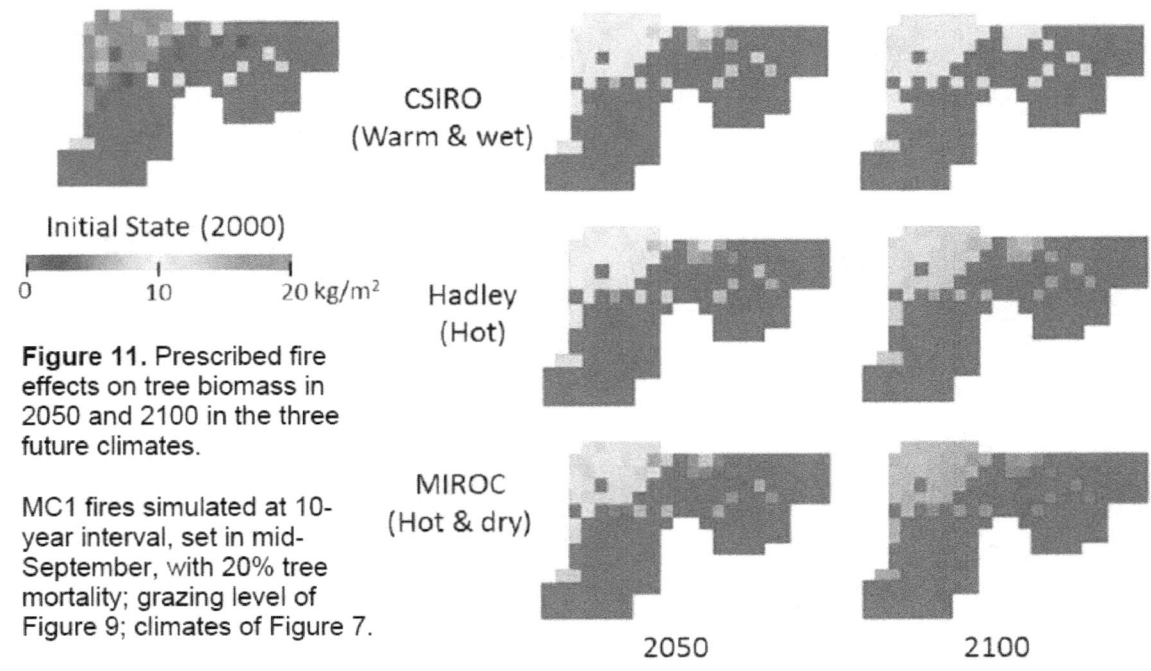

Initial State (2000)

0   10   20 kg/m²

CSIRO
(Warm & wet)

Hadley
(Hot)

MIROC
(Hot & dry)

2050   2100

Figure 11. Prescribed fire effects on tree biomass in 2050 and 2100 in the three future climates.

MC1 fires simulated at 10-year interval, set in mid-September, with 20% tree mortality; grazing level of Figure 9; climates of Figure 7.

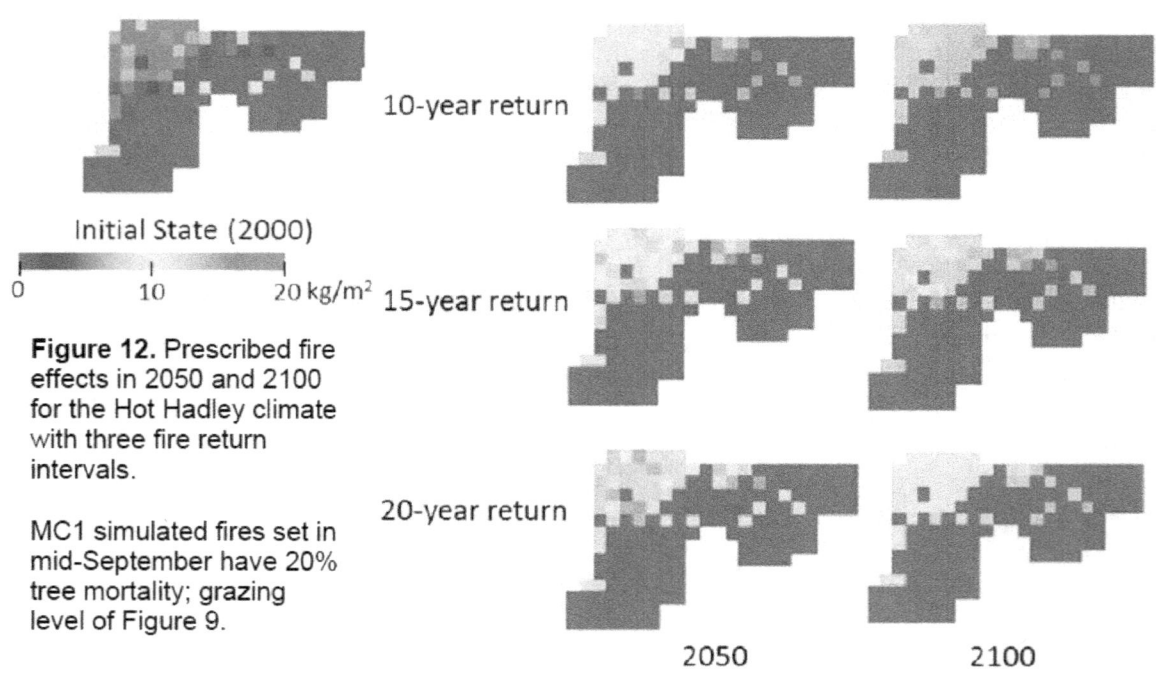

Initial State (2000)

0   10   20 kg/m²

10-year return

15-year return

20-year return

2050   2100

Figure 12. Prescribed fire effects in 2050 and 2100 for the Hot Hadley climate with three fire return intervals.

MC1 simulated fires set in mid-September have 20% tree mortality; grazing level of Figure 9.

28

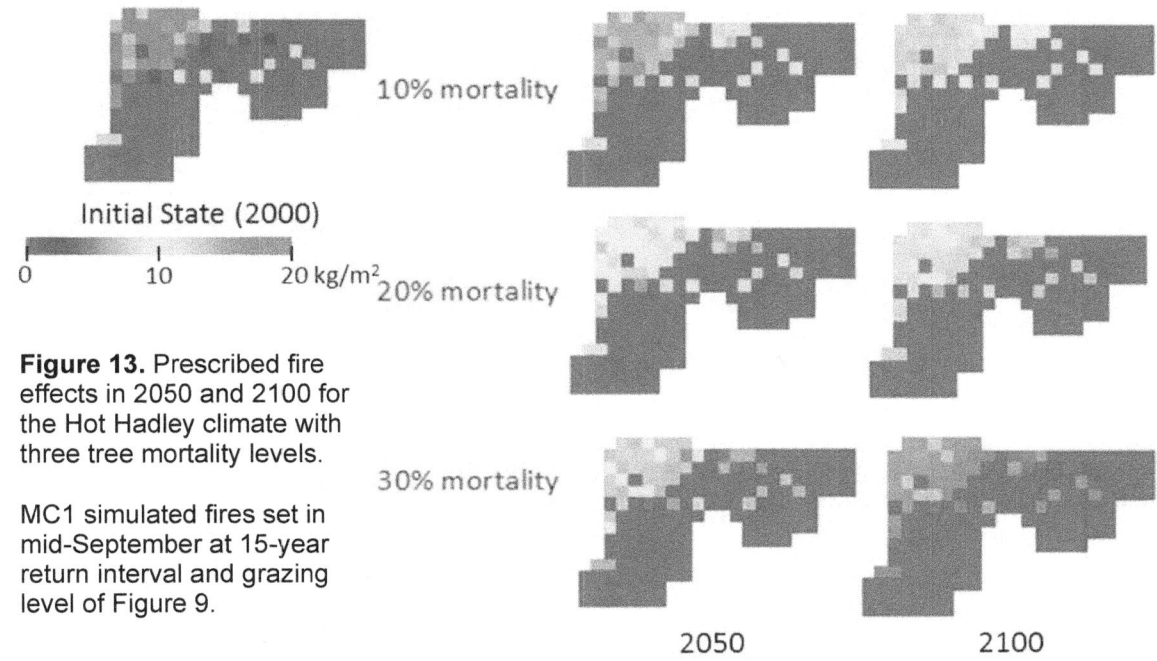

10% mortality

Initial State (2000)

0   10   20 kg/m² 20% mortality

Figure 13. Prescribed fire effects in 2050 and 2100 for the Hot Hadley climate with three tree mortality levels.

MC1 simulated fires set in mid-September at 15-year return interval and grazing level of Figure 9.

30% mortality

2050   2100

Future fire danger

Our simulation of fire effects is based on the assumption that wind speeds are at a general average level, with vegetation type-dependent reductions in this wind speed at the fire front, as described in "Vegetation-dependent Wind Speed" above. In addition, MC1 interpolates daily temperature and humidity from mean values per month, and sets one natural fire per year per cell where the fire thresholds are exceeded ("Fire Module", above). This approach limits the range in projected fire intensities, which in reality reach their maximum intensity on unusually hot and dry days of extreme winds during extended droughts. For example, the firestorms of Black Saturday, 2009 in Victoria Australia were associated with temperatures of up to 46° C, 6% humidity and winds that later reached 75 mph (http://en.wikipedia.org/wiki/Black_Saturday_bushfires).

Projected fire effects by MC1 (and in reality) are highly dependent on wind speed. For example, quadrupling wind speed from the standard 3.5 m/s to 14 m/s (31.3 mph) projects crown fires over the entire heavily forested NW section for all future climate scenarios, resulting in great reductions in woody biomass.

Although we cannot readily model the effects of stochastic variation in future wind speed, we can provide a qualitative assessment of the likelihood of severe fires in the future by examining the frequency distribution of MC1's fire danger indices. As the BUI is more reflective of longer-term drying of larger fuels and hence more accurately projected from the monthly climate inputs than is the FFMC, we chose this index to assess future fire danger. Figure 14 shows that the number of days that the BUI exceeds our fire ignition threshold increases with time for all three future climates. There is also a large divergence between scenarios, with the BUI exceeding our ignition threshold of 80 for an average of about 100 days per year by 2100 for MIROC vs. 60 and 20 days per year for Hadley and CSIRO, respectively, as assessed for the park headquarters cell. For the 20th century, the model predicts an average of 12 days per year, and maximum values of 87 and 76 days per year, respectively, for the two drought periods of the 1930's and 1950's. However, the difference in fire danger among future climate scenarios becomes apparent only after 2040.

Figure 14. Number of days per year that the build up index (BUI) exceeds 80, the fire ignition threshold for this index, in the 20th (top) and 21st (bottom) centuries.

Projections simulated by the dynamic global vegetation model MC1; for the 21st century simulations are under the climate scenarios shown in Figure 7.

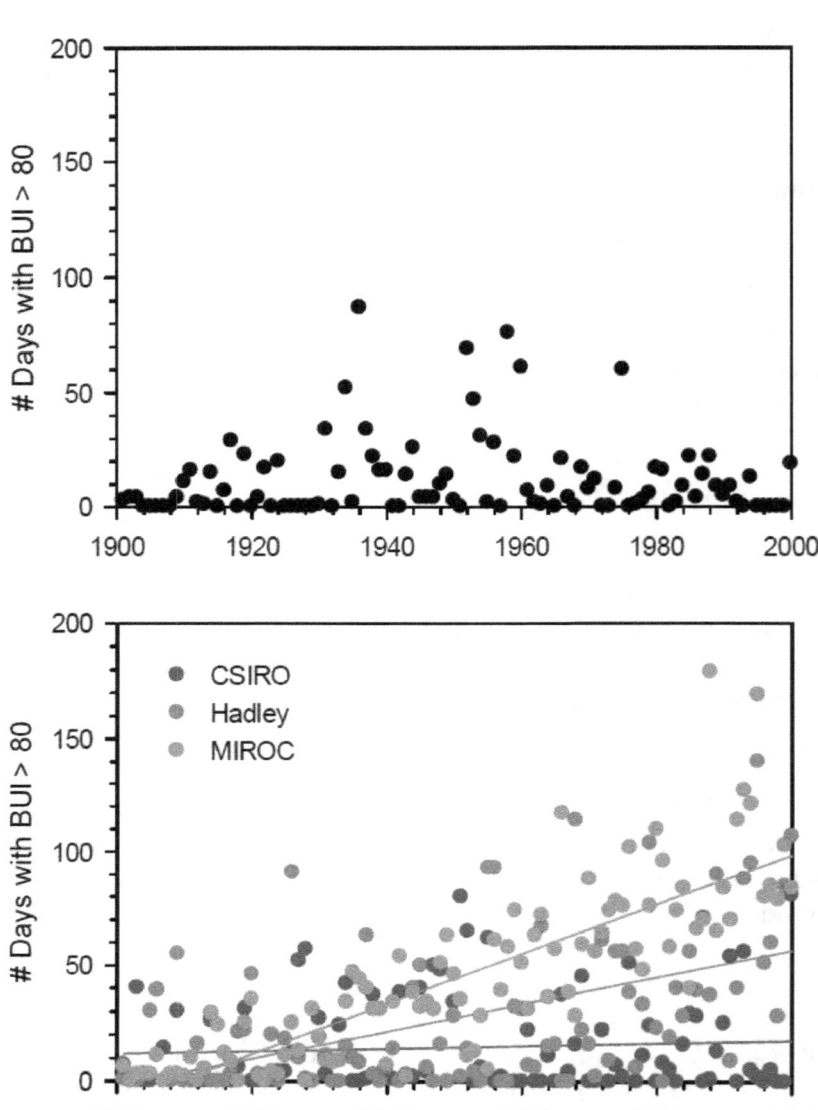

Future grassland production

Here we present results for the park headquarters cell, for which the average simulated LAI over the historical period is only 1.2% lower than that across all grassland cells. At the standard grazing level (30% removal), the maximum annual grass LAI varies substantially among years for all future climates, especially later in the 21st century, when it declines below 1 in a number of years for the hot and dry MIROC climate (Figure 15). Despite this, maximum grass LAI for MIROC is on average similar to that projected for the historical climate, whereas it is 12% and

30% higher for the Hadley and CSIRO climates, respectively. For all climates, there are substantive shifts in monthly trajectories of LAI over the 21st century, as illustrated in Figure 16, where we compare the 20 year monthly mean LAI for the last two decades of the future vs. historical periods. Here March-May LAI values for all future climates are substantially higher than under historical conditions, reflecting warmer springs and less limitation of growth by low temperatures (Figure 7, bottom left). LAI declines throughout the summer from its peak in June for Hadley and MIROC, but it peaks in July for both the CSIRO and historical climates. Roughly following precipitation patterns (Figure 7, bottom right), July-October LAIs are lower than historical for the Hadley and MIROC climates.

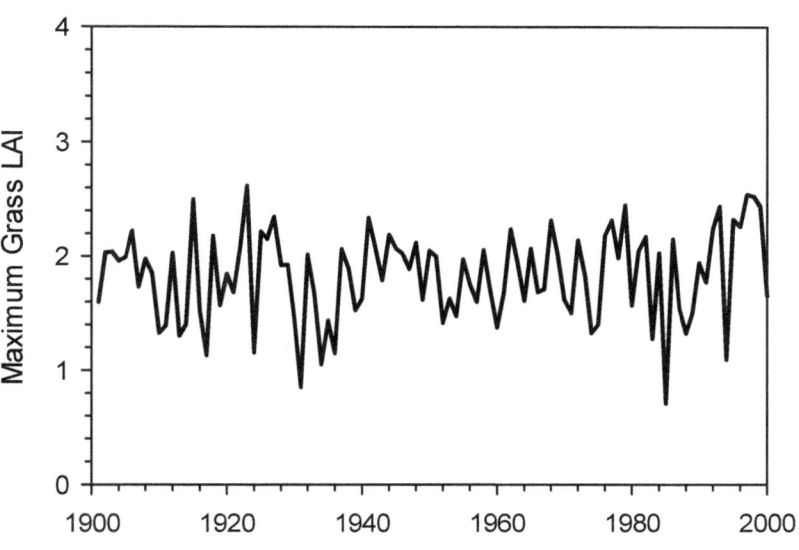

Figure 15. Annual maximum grass LAI (dimensionless) in the headquarters cell for the 20th (top) and 21st (bottom) centuries.

Simulations by the dynamic global vegetation model MC1 based on PRISM data (top) and the future climates of Figure 7 (bottom), using a 30% removal of growing season ANPP by grazers.

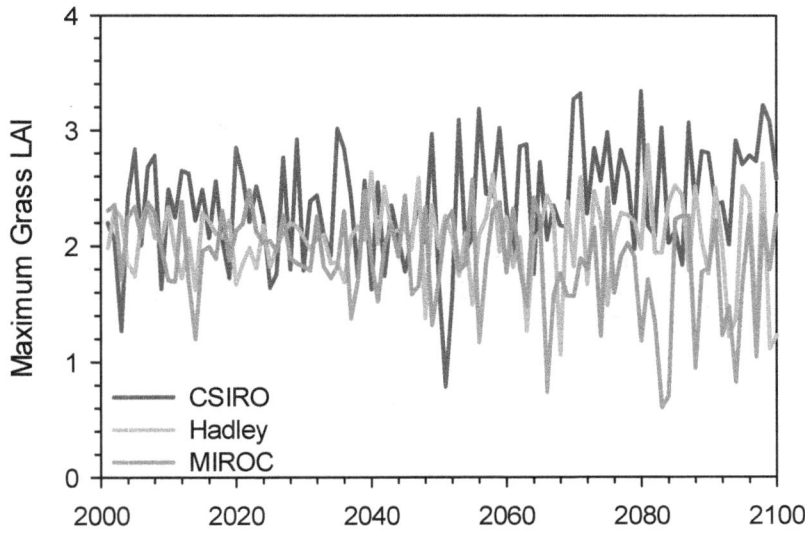

31

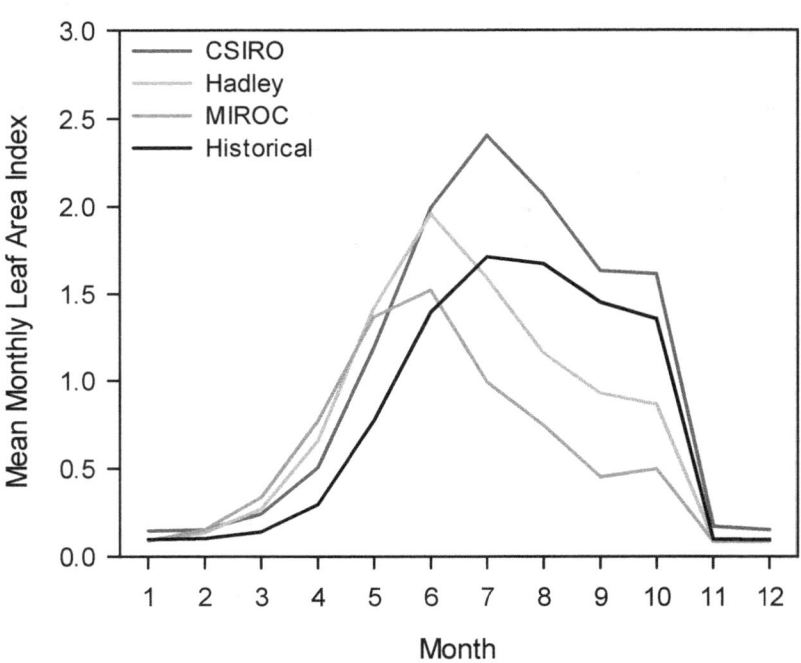

Figure 16. Mean monthly grass LAI for park headquarters cell for 2081-2100 (future climates) vs. 1981-2000 (historical climate).

MC1 simulations based on PRISM data and the future climates of Figure 7, with 30% removal of growing season ANPP by grazers.

We have not plotted monthly grass ANPP (i.e. forage production) because MC1 does not currently output monthly ANPP. However, during the April – September growing season, the change in monthly LAI should track the 70% of ANPP not removed by grazers minus monthly grass senescence. Thus, the future LAI patterns for Hadley and MIROC indicate relatively higher spring ANPP and lower summer ANPP than for the historical projection. Grassland production is also projected to shift from approximately equal contributions by C_3 and C_4 plants at present to a 60 to 80% contribution by C_4 plants in 2100, with this shift being more pronounced for Hadley and MIROC than for CSIRO (Figure 17). This shift is driven by increases in temperature, upon which MC1's calculation of the C3/C4 ratio is based.

Figure 17. Percentage of grassland production projected for C3 (cool season) grasses for the park headquarters cell for three climates.

MC1 simulations based on the future climates of Figure 7, 30% of growing-season ANPP removed by grazers.

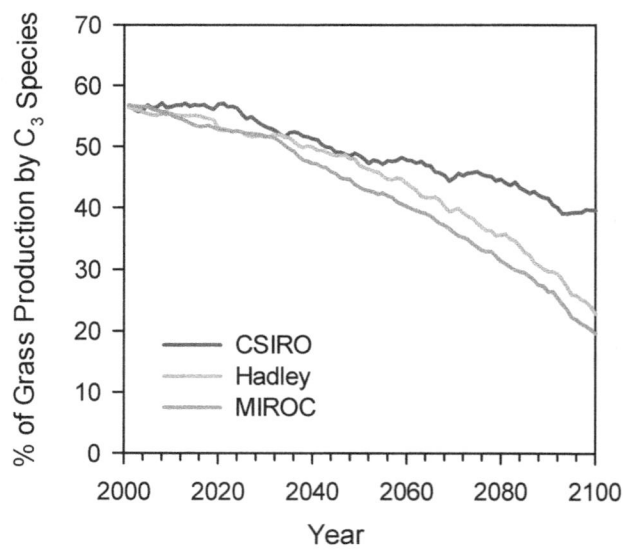

Grazing scenarios

Projected annual aboveground grass production (ANPP) differs little between the light (25% removal) grazing scenario and the moderate to heavy (50%) scenario, with the minor exception of the last two decades under MIROC (Figure 18). Grass production is generally lower during the second half of the 21st century for the hot and dry MIROC climate and higher but more variable for the warm and wet CSIRO climate.

The very high (70%) grazing scenario greatly reduces ANPP, particularly in the latter half of the 21st century, most notably for MIROC (Figure 18). This future climate results in considerably less projected forage uptake by grazers than does the 50% removal scenario. Here

$$forage\ uptake = removal\ fraction * ANPP * uptake\ efficiency \qquad (6)$$

where uptake efficiency is less than one due to trampling and grazing by non-target herbivores, including insects. The 70% removal scenario is higher than grazing scenarios envisioned by park managers for the whole park, but they might occur in a drought period if herd size was not adjusted accordingly, and they are relevant to areas with prairie dog colonies. There is some increase in inter-year variation in production under all three future climates, so this result supports the adoption of somewhat more conservative herd management, particularly after 2030. At present, no explicit effects of grazers on soil erosion and structure are included in MC1.

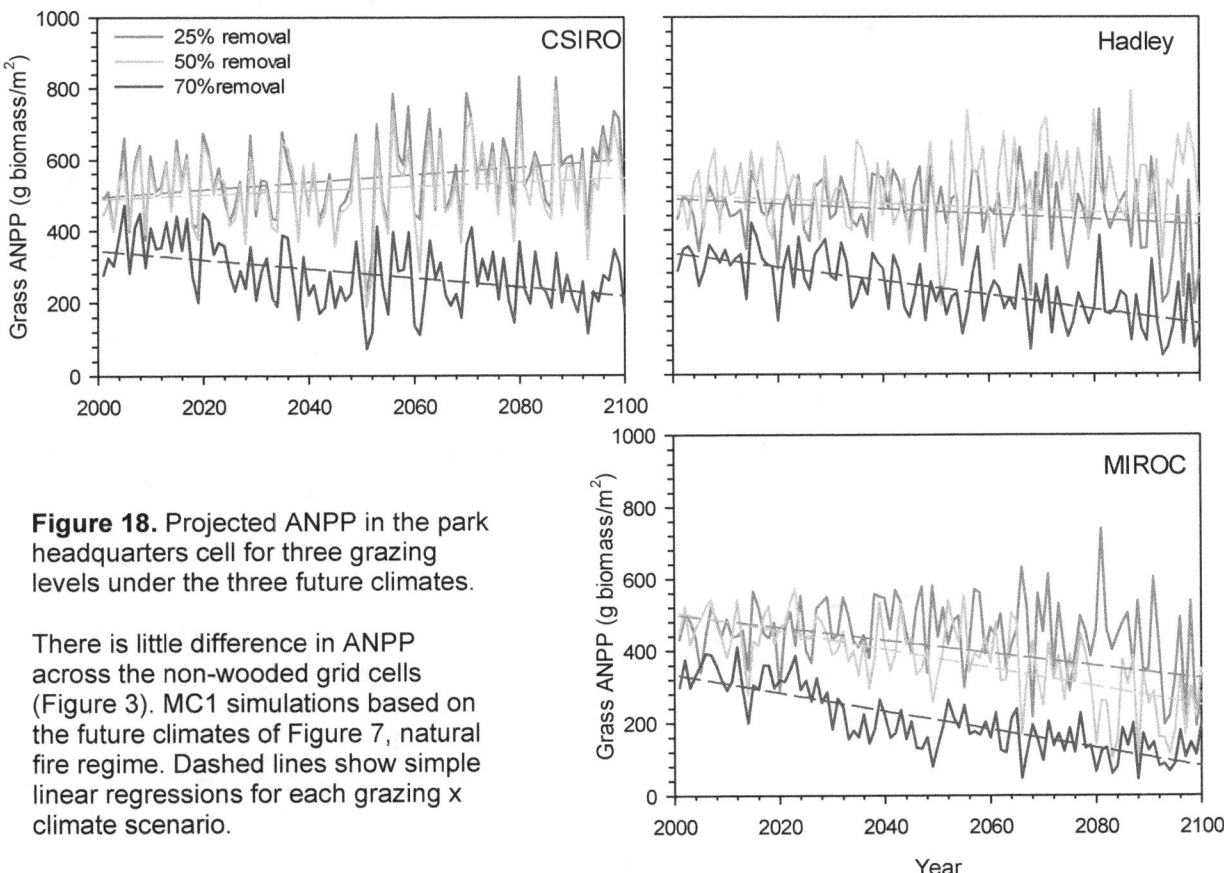

Figure 18. Projected ANPP in the park headquarters cell for three grazing levels under the three future climates.

There is little difference in ANPP across the non-wooded grid cells (Figure 3). MC1 simulations based on the future climates of Figure 7, natural fire regime. Dashed lines show simple linear regressions for each grazing x climate scenario.

Fire Scenarios

Park-wide grass productivity is quite similar for a reasonable prescribed fire scenario (10-year return interval, 20% tree mortality) and the natural fire scenario (Figure 19) because in both of these cases fires are frequent enough to keep trees out of grassland cells but not severe enough to convert forested cells to grassland. However, fire suppression results in gradual woody invasion of many of the grassland cells, thereby lowering the whole-park grass ANPP as compared to the other fire scenarios for all three future climates (Figure 19). Grassland fires temporarily reduce surface litter, which stimulates grass production as simulated by MC1, accentuating the difference in ANPP between the fire suppression and non-suppression projections.

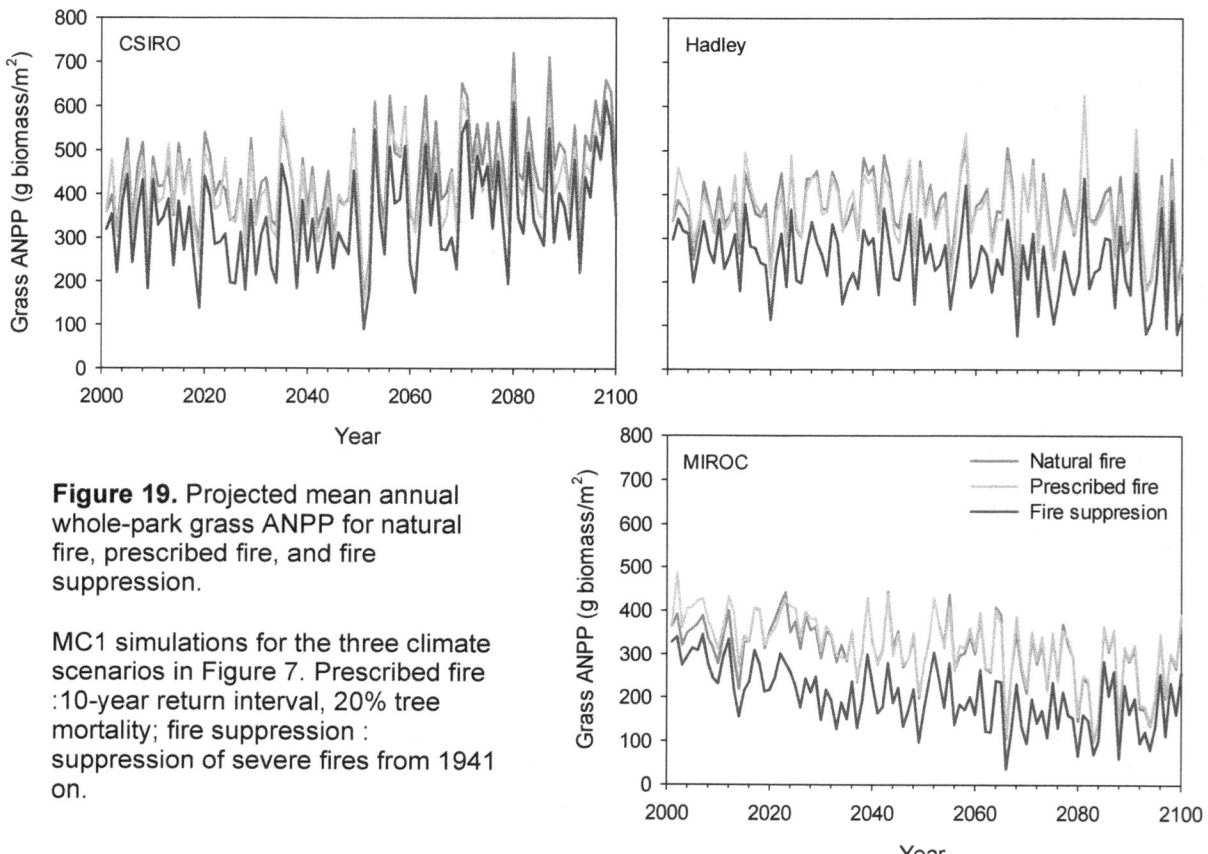

Figure 19. Projected mean annual whole-park grass ANPP for natural fire, prescribed fire, and fire suppression.

MC1 simulations for the three climate scenarios in Figure 7. Prescribed fire :10-year return interval, 20% tree mortality; fire suppression : suppression of severe fires from 1941 on.

Projected CO2 effects on grass ANPP

The direct effects of CO_2 on plant productivity and transpiration may become increasingly important as CO_2 concentrations rise. Projections of future grass productivity for the headquarters cell with these effects turned off show that CO_2 effects act to sustain production for the Hadley climate, increase production for CSIRO and blunt the decline in production for the hot and dry MIROC climate (Figure 20). The effects of doubling CO_2 before 2100 are particularly great for MIROC, likely due to the CO_2-mediated increase in water use efficiency for this very droughty scenario. Mean projected grass ANPP for 2091-2100 is reduced by 17% for CSIRO and Hadley and 27% for MIROC, when CO_2 effects are turned off. Note that although precipitation changes little for the Hadley climate, projected ANPP declines substantially without CO_2 effects, due to a large increase in PET that is associated with the substantial increase in temperature and vapor pressure deficit over the 21st century.

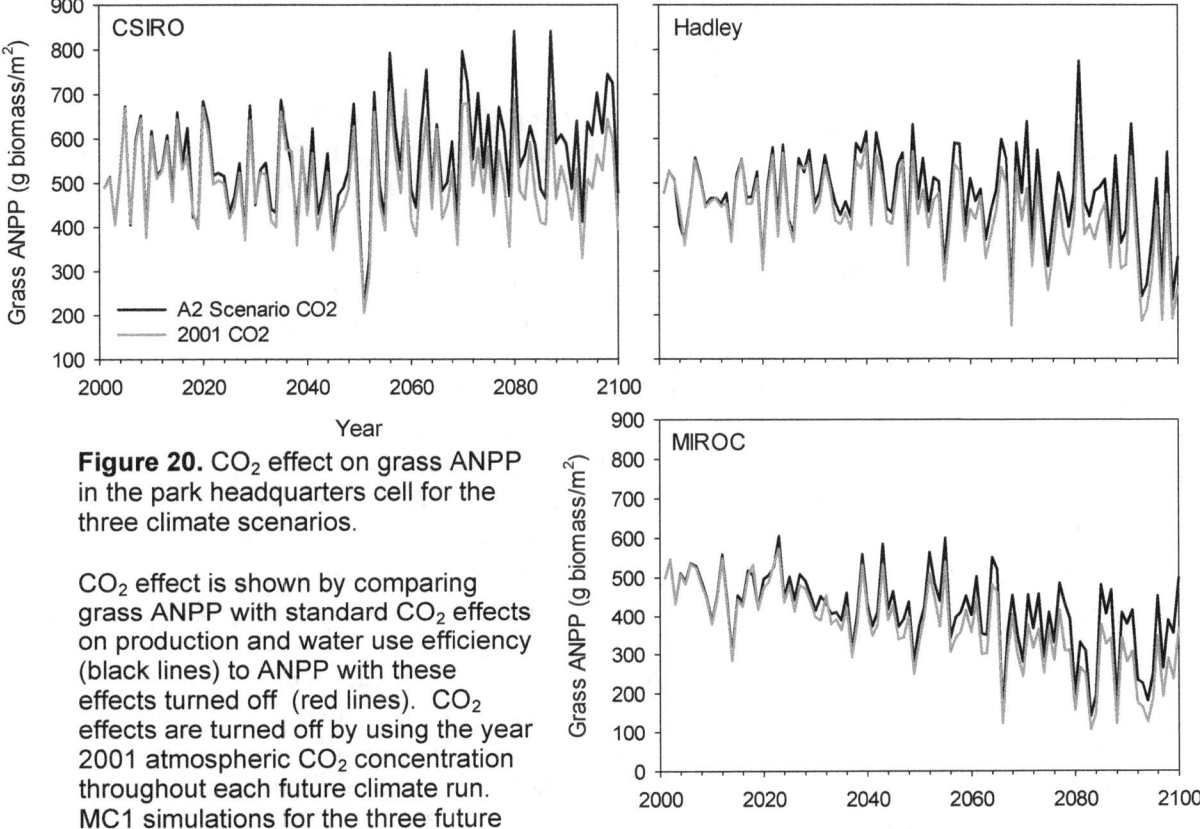

Figure 20. CO_2 effect on grass ANPP in the park headquarters cell for the three climate scenarios.

CO_2 effect is shown by comparing grass ANPP with standard CO_2 effects on production and water use efficiency (black lines) to ANPP with these effects turned off (red lines). CO_2 effects are turned off by using the year 2001 atmospheric CO_2 concentration throughout each future climate run. MC1 simulations for the three future climate scenarios of Figure 7.

Discussion

Our application of the MC1 model to Wind Cave National Park approximates the current proportions of wooded areas and grasslands and the greater concentration of trees in the northwest section of the Park, with exceptions regarding the fine scale mosaic of trees and grass (Figure 2). Projections for three 21st century climate scenarios indicate persistence of wooded areas, given our standard assumption of average wind speeds. However, the greater frequency of days of high fire danger, particularly in the latter half of the 21st century (Figure 14), implies a greater chance that fire ignition and high winds will occur together, resulting in crown fires. Our evaluation of management scenarios suggest that, broadly speaking, current park resources can be protected well into the future, depending on the skill of park managers in using fire and controlling herd sizes.

The projected distributions of forests and grasslands are largely determined by the simulated fire frequencies and tree growth rates across the WICA domain. The somewhat hotter and drier conditions in the eastern and southernmost areas result in higher simulated fire frequencies and somewhat lower forest growth rates. In these areas, the simulated trees are young and small with low crown base heights, making them susceptible to death by crown fires that reduce tree biomass to a very low level during the long model spinup phase. In contrast, the lower simulated fire frequency and somewhat higher forest growth rates in the northwest portion of the park result in low-mortality surface fires that allow the forests to approach their maximum (production-limited) biomass during the spinup period. Thus, sharp boundaries between forest and grassland are simulated, depending on whether or not trees grow tall enough to survive fire.

We projected no change from pure conifer forests in the future because the tree type was constrained to evergreen needleleaf for the future simulations (see "Biogeography" above). However, a wetter and warmer future (the CSIRO scenario) could greatly increase the deciduous broadleaf forest component if recruitment is not limited by other, non-climatic factors such as seed sources and browsing (projections not shown).

Comparison to Other Future Projections
Wind Cave National Park projections
MC1 was first applied to WICA by Bachelet et al. (2000), who simulated current and future vegetation dynamics, focusing on the prairie-forest balance, over a 2.5 x 5 km domain in the northwest section of the park with interpolated topography-dependent climate inputs (Daly 2000). This fine-scale, 50 x 50 m grid cell application captured the topography-dependent distribution of current forests. Here forest occurred on unburned or rarely burned cells associated with lower potential evapotranspiration that was driven by lower temperatures, particularly on upper north-facing slopes. In our current application, forest occurs primarily on the cooler, higher elevation cells, which also have slightly higher precipitation. Here fire ignition frequency is lower and tree production is a bit higher, allowing for sufficient tree growth between fires to prevent crown fire during the long spinup period. Both applications project widespread fire in 1936, a year of severe drought, with extremely high summer temperatures. However, Bachelet et al (2000) projected an 80% decrease in woody biomass from this fire, whereas we project a ~15% biomass decrease. This difference reflects our changes to the fire module to more accurately represent presettlement surface fires in the southern Black Hills.

For the future, Bachelet et al. (2000) projected an initial buildup in woody biomass that declined by 90% due to two years of widespread fire in the 2030s. This result was based on the HADCM2SUL climate scenario, which projects a 4° C increase in average temperature and little change in precipitation over the 21st century for WICA. We projected large increases in future fire frequency, but less severe effects per fire for futures that are warmer than that projected by HADCM2SUL, in the cases of Hadley and MIROC future climates. With the earlier fire module formulation, forest would remain at WICA in the future only if the fire ignition thresholds were raised substantially. Even then, the future rise in the fire danger indices would still have yielded widespread crown fires. We regard our formulation of the fine fuel loads that strongly influence crown fire occurrence as more realistic than the earlier formulation, but also recognize that more realistic variable wind speeds would result in the projection of more crown fires.

Future fire effects in the West
Other projections of fire over the western USA by DGVMs generally predict an increase in future fire frequency and area burned, but typically without a decline in in the overall area occupied by woody vegetation types (Bachelet et al. 2003; Lenihan et al. 2008; Rogers et al. 2011). Increases in fire effects have also been predicted by statistical fire models fit to historical climate data. Litschert et al. (2012) predicted a 10-fold increase in mean annual burned area from 2011 to 2070 for the Southern Rockies Ecoregion, based on the Hadley CM3 A2 climate projection. Westerling et al. (2011) predicted large increases in fire frequency over the 21st century for the Greater Yellowstone Ecosystem. This area is characterized by infrequent severe fires, with a return interval of 100 – 300 years. The regionally averaged return interval was predicted to decline to 10 years or less by 2080 based on future climates from 3 GCMs under the A2 emissions scenario, a change likely to threaten the persistence of current conifer species there (Westerling et al. 2011).

Species range projections
Our prediction of the persistence of ponderosa pine forests throughout the 21st century differs from projections of the future range of this species based on empirical relationships between species presence-absence and historical climate (also known as climate envelope relationships). Both Shafer et al. (2001) and Rehfeldt et al. (2006) project a contraction in the range of ponderosa pine that excludes the Black Hills by the end of the 21st century. Also, based on random forests multiple-regression tree models, Rehfeld et al. (2006) found that for two downscaled and averaged GCM projections[4] the climate profile for ponderosa pine would exclude WICA in the 2030s and all of the Black Hills in the 2090s.

This finding justifies concern over the future of ponderosa pine in the park, but its implications for the next century are uncertain because empirical models do not address the mechanisms and time scales over which climate influences species ranges. In contrast to the predictions of species range models, Canham (2012) projected only modest shifts in simulated tree species distributions over the 21st century for eastern temperate forests, despite an increase of 6°C in mean annual temperature over this period. This result was based on a spatially explicit forest dynamics model, which included species-specific effects of competition and climate on growth and survival of all life stages, as parameterized from US forest inventory and analysis (FIA) data. Canham (2012)

---

[4] HadCM3 and CGCM2 with a 1%/yr increase in greenhouse gases after 1990.

concluded that over the next 50 years, introduced pests and pathogens and tree harvest regimes are likely to have greater effects than climate change on eastern forests. However, this conclusion applies to a substantially wetter region than the southern Black Hills.

In the case of Rehfeldt and colleagues' (2006) analysis of ponderosa pine, the most important classification variables were the minimum number of degree days below 0° C, the annual moisture index (= degree days > 5 ° C / mean annual precipitation) and the ratio of annual temperature differential to growing season precipitation. Of these variables, the cold temperature requirement and/or the moisture index are most likely involved in the forecast of unsuitable future climates for ponderosa pine in the Black Hills. The temperature requirement might be related to seed germination, whereas the annual moisture index could be related to the survival of young, shallow-rooted seedlings as well as mature trees, made more susceptible to bark beetle attacks. Allen and Breshears (1998) observed a shift in the ponderosa pine – pinion pine-juniper ecotone boundary at a site in northern New Mexico, which they attributed to 1950s drought effects exacerbated by bark beetles.

Fire is a key regulator of the abundance and distribution of many species that is not addressed in species range models. Fire suppression has resulted in a proliferation of fire-sensitive trees and reduced the regeneration of many fire-dependent plants throughout eastern North America (Nowacki and Abrams 2008). Using a process-based DGVM, Bond et al. (2005) projected a doubling of forest cover in a world without fire. Our model prediction that ponderosa pine would invade park grasslands without fire is in agreement with current pine seedling distributions at Wind Cave. Also, in an extensive study of seed source effects on performance, ponderosa pine seedlings from the Black Hills and Rocky Mountain foothills showed high 15-year survival across the northern, central and southern Great Plains (Van Haverbeke 1986). Although most of the trial sites in this study received more precipitation than WICA, one (Alliance, NE) was drier and slightly warmer than the park headquarters.

Thus, Black Hills ponderosa pines can survive far beyond their current localities, though their limits with respect to warmer and drier climes are uncertain. It is plausible that frequent grass fires prevented the presettlement expansion of ponderosa pine into the lower and warmer prairies to the east of WICA. Here the combination of somewhat drier fuels and lack of topographic fire breaks would have increased fire frequency. An alternative hypothesis is that low infiltration rates in the Pierre shale-derived "gumbo" clay soils to the east of the Black Hills restrict the growth of ponderosa pines there. For example, soils of the Pierre series have permeability rates of less than 0.06 inches/hr (USDA Natural Resources Conservation Service 1996). Soils of the Pierre, Kyle and Samsil series that make up gumbo soils comprise 30% of the prairie parts of Custer and Pennington counties as mapped by the Soil Conservation Service to the east of Wind Cave, but have not been recorded within the Park itself (USDA Natural Resources Conservation Service 1990; 1996). Whereas gumbo soils may exclude ponderosa pines further to the east, the presettlement fire regime has likely had a substantive role in excluding pines from much of the eastern part of the Park. In sum, current species boundaries may in part reflect the effect of climate on fire regimes, as well as correlations between climate, soils and topography (warmer and drier in flat lowlands with few firebreaks).

Other uncertainties in the interpretation of empirical species models involve the time required for species ranges to adjust to new climates in the face of uncertain patterns in future land use, as well as the large differences between past and present disturbance regimes and connectivity of natural vegetation. All of these influence plant survival and migration. The historical ranges of long-lived trees reflect not only the migration of species over recent millennia and the suitability of climate for establishment and survival over past centuries, but also competitors, pests, pathogens and disturbance regimes including fire. As noted by Oliver and Larson (1996), trees often grow best in moist, well-drained, sandy clay loam soils, but species grow where they can compete successfully, not where they can grow best. More importantly, effects of elevated CO_2 on growth and water use efficiency are not incorporated in empirical species models, but they can significantly affect the resilience of forests to changing climate.

Uncertainties

There are multiple dimensions of uncertainty in projecting ecosystem responses to an uncertain future climate. These dimensions include the local climate projections, which are affected by uncertainties in climate simulations and the downscaling methods used (Hostetler et al. 2011; Maraun et al. 2010), as well as unavoidable uncertainties in the greenhouse gas projections driving the climate models. However, the latter uncertainties seem to be more about the rate of increase in greenhouse gases rather than the direction of change. Since the actual rate of increase has been at least as high as the A2 scenario we used for our future climates (Le Quéré et al. 2009), effects on ecosystems are likely, but their extent and timing are unclear. Here we focus on uncertainties in the projections of DGVMs using a 30-arc second resolution and monthly climate inputs, with emphasis on the application of MC1 to WICA.

We first assess our three future climate scenarios as compared to the ensemble projections of GCMs for North America presented in chapter 11 of IPCC (2007). Figure 11.12 of IPCC (2007) presents broad isotherms of temperature and precipitation change over North America, as given by the ensemble mean of 21 GCMs under the A1B anthropogenic emission scenario. From this figure we determined the approximate ensemble mean changes for WICA for the A1B emission scenario as shown in Table 1 for 2080-2099 vs. 1980-1999 and compared it to our three climate projections for the same future period vs. PRISM recent historical. Table 1 shows that Hadley is close to the ensemble mean for precipitation and CSIRO is close to the ensemble mean for temperature increase. However, our climate projections were made under the more severe A2 emission scenario, which results in an ensemble mean global surface temperature increase that is 15-20% greater than that under the A1B emission scenario for the comparison period of Table 1 (IPCC 2007 – Figure TS.32). This difference suggests that the ensemble mean temperature increase for WICA would lie roughly midway between that projected by CSIRO and Hadley, had the comparison been made using the same A2 emission scenario for all GCMs. Considering both temperature and precipitation projections together, the Hadley climate projection thus appears close to the GCM ensemble mean for WICA, with the other two projections bracketing this mean with respect to heat and drought.

Table 1. Comparison of projected change in temperature and precipitation for the three future climates in Figure 7 to the mean change projected by an ensemble of GCMs.

Change is between the averages for 2080-2099 and 1980-1999. Values for the individual climate models are for the park headquarters cell (A2 emission scenario) and were calculated as the difference between 2080-2099 future projections and 1980-1999 historical PRISM data. Values for the ensemble are for the region including Wind Cave National Park; means averaged over 21 GCMs and the A1B emission scenario (which is less severe than the A2 scenario) were used for both periods and the differences mapped as isotherms over North America in Figure 11.12 of IPCC (2007).

GCM and Emission Scenario	Temperature Change (°C)	Precipitation Change (%)
CSIRO A2	3.8	16
Hadley A2	5.6	-1
MIROC A2	6.8	-24
Ensemble mean A1B	3.5 – 4.0	0 – 5

Regarding uncertainties in DGVMs, the projection of climate change effects is an endeavor that is continuously undergoing development both in the downscaling of global climate projections and in the improvement of the vegetation models. The difference between our current projections and the previous application of MC1 to Wind Cave (see "Wind Cave National Park Projections" above) provides an illustration of this model development. Nonetheless, current DGVMs continue to underrepresent lags in species migration, pests and pathogens, invasive plant species and human management activities (Lenihan et al. 2008). An intrinsic challenge in modeling native vegetation is the huge range in spatial and temporal scales involved. It is relatively straightforward to project short-term crop production as affected by year-to-year variation in weather, but more challenging when disturbance-driven changes in lifeform are involved.

In our judgment, future fire effects and the influence of extreme events on plant survival and regeneration are major areas of uncertainty in our projections. These factors can drive sudden, large-scale changes, particularly along ecotones. Our simulation of fire effects is constrained by the interpolation of monthly climate inputs, which do not include day-to-day fluctuations in temperature, humidity and wind speed, and by the ignition algorithm, which sets a maximum of one fire per year per cell on the day when the ignition thresholds are first exceeded. It is critical that managers recognize these limitations and understand that the projected changes in high fire danger imply increased chances for extreme fire weather that could have a significant influence on future vegetation not captured by our simulations.

In addition, the relatively small geographic range in mean temperature and precipitation across WICA required that small changes in simulated fine fuel loads or other aspects of the fire parameterization have large effects on the simulated proportions of forest and grassland in order to properly simulate the observed ecotone. In reality, spatial heterogeneity in fuel loads, topography and ignition sources will introduce greater spatial and temporal variability in fire and undoubtedly produce a more complex pattern of fire behavior than simulated here (Baker 2009). For example, the greater topographic ruggedness in the currently forested areas of WICA may also contribute to tree survival by providing refuges from fire from which trees can reinvade after episodes of greater wildfires.

Our prediction of higher fire frequency in the future is in general agreement with predictions for the western USA derived from statistical fire models ("Future Fire Effects in the West", above), but the projections of fire severity are more uncertain. The intensification of fire effects when a surface fire crowns and the sensitivity of crowning to local fuel distribution and wind speed make the mechanistic prediction of fire severity extremely challenging. The complex topography and vegetation of the park makes it unlikely that a single fire would crown over most of the wooded area, but the extent of the largest wildfire over the past 25 years (13% of park area) suggests that substantial tree cover could be removed.

MC1 currently simulates constant tree mortality rates for each tree type, depending on user-specified parameters. As the life, death and species identity of individual tree cohorts are not simulated, there is no simulation of seedling establishment. The scalar that calculates the effect of tree LAI on tree production sets a minimum value for LAI (very low for WICA) that ensures some tree production in all cases (see "Tree Production", above), so prolonged drought effects on tree cohort establishment are not clearly represented. For old, undisturbed forests, tree biomass declines during periods of low productivity (typically associated with drought) when mortality effects exceed growth, but again, prolonged drought does not produce relatively abrupt mortality of trees due to drought. Fire is the only simulated mechanism causing abrupt removal of live tree biomass.

Combinations of drought stress, pests, pathogens and competitors may cause increased tree mortality (Fan et al. 2011, 2012). Allen and Breshears (1998) documented a rapid drought-induced shift in the ecotone between ponderosa pine-dominated woodland and pinyon-juniper woodland in a wilderness section of Bandelier National Monument. The shift was caused by the death of ponderosa pines along the ecotone during a severe drought in the 1950s, likely exacerbated by competition with coexisting pinyon pines and junipers and a concurrent bark beetle outbreak. Ponderosa pines have not re-established, perhaps due in part to heavy subsequent erosion, likely triggered by loss of herbaceous cover during the drought and overgrazing by feral burros (Davenport et al. 1998).

Adult ponderosa pines are deep rooted and have high drought tolerance (Niinemets and Valladares 2006). However, drought lessens their ability to withstand bark beetle attacks (Negròn et al. 2009). Prolonged droughts allow bark beetle populations to reach epidemic levels and cause heavy regional mortality of ponderosa pine and other pine species, particularly among stressed trees of dense stands (Negròn et al. 2009; Bentz et al. 2010). During such epidemics, the beetles may attack in sufficient numbers to overwhelm the defenses of even widely-spaced, vigorous trees.

Over the past decade, a severe outbreak of mountain pine beetles has impacted large areas of pine forests in the Black Hills and the front ranges of Colorado and Wyoming. On Colorado timberlands, this outbreak has contributed to an estimated mortality of 21,000,000 and 142,000,000 cubic feet per year for ponderosa and lodgepole pine respectively, from 2002 – 2009 (Colorado State Forest Service 2011). Nonetheless, ponderosa pine showed an estimated net volume increase of 16,000,000 cubic feet per year, though lodgepole pine declined by 71,000,000 cubic feet per year during this period. Thus, for ponderosa pine, the statewide beetle caused mortality did not exceed the volume growth of surviving trees, though particular areas declined greatly.

The most severe beetle outbreak in the Black Hills was that of 1894-1908, which killed 80,000,000 to 170,000,000 cubic feet of timber (Oliver and Ryker 1991), about 5-10% of the current wood volume on the Black Hills National Forest (DeBlander 2002). Major outbreaks also occurred in the 1940s and 1970s (http://www.fs.usda.gov/detail/blackhills/landmanagement/ ?cid=stelprdb5113978). The current outbreak began in the northern Black Hills in 1996 and has persisted and expanded through the present (2012) (http://www.beatthebeetles.com/docs/ blackhills-beetle-epidemic-2011.pdf, D. Swanson, NPS Northern Great Plains Fire Ecology Program, personal communication). This outbreak is second only to that of 1894-1908 in number of trees killed, but has had little effect on the forest at WICA.

MC1 captures the effect of drought conditions on tree growth. For example, MC1 simulated below-average tree production associated with below-average precipitation and above-average temperature in 2000-2007 at WICA. However, the model does not currently translate these stress effects into simulated beetle outbreaks. Nonetheless, the increased likelihood of more severe droughts, due in part to higher evaporative demand associated with higher temperatures (Figure 7), could play a role in future climate-beetle interactions at WICA provided that tree densities are high enough to be conducive to high beetle populations. Increased water use efficiency associated with elevated CO_2 will likely reduce the impacts of drought on tree vigor (Wyckoff and Bowers 2010), but the degree to which this will occur is unknown. Other climatic factors that will influence mountain pine beetle and other insect impacts on trees include increasing minimum temperatures, shorter durations of low temperatures, and earlier and later occurrences of warm temperatures, which affect winter mortality, brood synchronization, and symbionts of the insects (Schmid et al. 1993; Bentz et al. 2010). In addition, elevated CO_2 tends to reduce plant tissue nitrogen concentrations, which may slow the growth of beetle larvae (Bentz et al. 2010).

Management Implications
Monitoring
Given the unavoidable uncertainties in future projections of climate change effects on Park resources, monitoring of range quality and species composition, and in wooded areas, measurements of tree density and growth and seedling abundance are of great importance. Long-term drought has been found to favor short-lived, ruderal herbs in shortgrass prairie (Evans et al. 2011). Drought severity will vary with slope, aspect and soil depth and texture over a finer scale than this study's 800 m grid projections. Grazing intensity is quite variable over the park (Wind Cave National Park Division of Resource Management, 2009) and may interact with drought impacts in affecting range quality. Continued monitoring of forage production and species composition over the ecological site types already used by the park will help evaluate the spectrum of climate/grazing impacts at WICA.

The ability of ponderosa pines to withstand bark beetle attacks is inversely related to degree of crowding by neighbors, as indicated by stand basal area, and is positively correlated with diameter growth rate (Zausen et al. 2005; Fettig et al. 2007). Thus, an assessment of tree basal area would provide a helpful baseline for monitoring the health of wooded areas. This could be accomplished through the establishment of permanent plots along line transects in a stratified random fashion. However, small plot measurements will have high residual errors due to the chance inclusion or exclusion of a few large trees, and so will overestimate the true variation in basal area. Circular plots with marked centers and tree inclusion determined by laser rangefinder should prove an accurate and efficient sampling method (Lindsay et al. 1958). Cores taken from a subset of trees of similar diameter would provide measures of recent growth rates (Zausen et al. 2005). There have been some concerns that cores may allow pathogens that have been walled off by trees to invade unaffected tissues, but cores need only penetrate the outer sapwood to assess the past decade of growth. Recoring trees at decadal intervals would provide a measure of any shifts in growth rate and tree vigor.

Invasive pests and pathogens are a major threat to plants with or without climate change. For example, chestnut blight and the hemlock wooly adelgid have caused major changes in the species composition of eastern forests. Dutch elm disease has markedly reduced the lifespan and stature of elms, though they still regenerate in native forests. In addition to monitoring bark beetle densities, it would be helpful to monitor for other invasive pests and pathogens as they are reported in South Dakota, whether or not they are aided by climate change. In the case of invasive plants with bird-dispersed seeds, such as buckthorn and juniper, early eradication of local infestations is much easier than battling them "after the horse has gotten out of the barn" (Rejmánek and Pitcairn 2002). Wind Cave National Park has benefited by its isolation from more populated areas from whence invasive species like these are likely to spread, making early eradication of invasives more feasible. The small population sizes of hardwood species at WICA may also provide an advantage in making them less apparent to deadly invasive insects, such as the emerald ash borer.

Fire management
Our simulations support the current use of fire to maintain grasslands and reduce fuel loads and tree densities in wooded areas. However, the relative importance of these functions of fire will vary among climate scenarios. Trees may be more resistant to bark beetle attacks under the warm and wet CSIRO future than the hot and dry MIROC future, necessitating less reduction in tree densities to maintain forest health in the former case. Greater proliferation of ladder fuels is also likely under moister conditions – and in the absence of fire, more vigorous invasions of grasslands by trees. Adjustments in fire management strategies will thus be required as the direction of regional climate change and its ecosystem impacts become clearer and as future projections are improved. In sum, the simulations suggest that climate alone will not eliminate ponderosa pine from the park in this century (but see 4.1.3), but lack of prescribed fires or other means of reducing forest density and increasing crown base height could severely reduce it.

Our model projections of a homogenization of forest biomass after repeated controlled burns (Figures 11-13) may be unrealistic, due to our convenient but unrealistic assumption that managers can control fire to produce uniform mortality rates across landscapes. Substantial between-plot variation in mortality has been recorded following prescribed fires at WICA (data provided by A. Symstad). The vagaries of wind and fuel loads that are not in our model will produce heterogeneous fire effects, thus contributing to heterogeneous forest structure. Substantial spatial heterogeneity for Black Hills forests at the time of Euro-American settlement was inferred by Brown and Cook (2006). Because MC1 calculates fire effects for a tree of average size based on stand biomass, it does not capture the reduction in fire danger due the removal of saplings and shrubs by surface fires (though it does simulate the burning of surface litter and standing dead grass). This removal of ladder fuels is an additional benefit of prescribed fires.

Maintaining current or somewhat lower mean basal area over the wooded areas of the park via prescribed burns should make the region more resistant to bark beetle outbreaks than would a fire suppression only approach. Although MC1 projects the eventual afforestation of the whole Park without fire, little increase in forest biomass of current forests is simulated because the long model spinup results in a late successional state for forests and because we needed to simulate low-mortality surface fires to match the forest – grass ecotone. However, much of the wooded area of Wind Cave may not be near equilibrium, due to past fire (and perhaps logging) and tree expansion into grasslands following fire suppression. Thus, it is likely that stand basal area would increase without fire over most of the wooded areas. Decadal surveys of overall stand basal area and its heterogeneity, as well as tree diameter distributions would be highly useful in assessing and adjusting the fire management program.

Our projections of higher fire danger for all three future climates imply that more resources will be required both to suppress fire ignitions during times of high fire danger and to maintain the ability to conduct prescribed fires at times when they are likely to have the desired effects. More resources for monitoring fire effects and ecosystem health under a changing climate would also be desirable.

Finally, given the potential for climatic factors to limit ponderosa pine growth, reproduction, and ultimately survival in ways not captured by MC1 (e.g., Rehfeldt et al. 2006), a cautionary approach to fire management with respect to maintaining ponderosa pine in the park may be appropriate. In other words, if monitoring like that suggested above or climate trends indicate that the conditions are becoming less conducive to ponderosa pine recruitment than desired, managers might consider postponing scheduled prescribed burns until a (presumably rare) young cohort reaches a fire-resistant height.

Grazing management

Our future simulations projected three diverging trends of total forage production over time, depending on the climate scenario. Consistent across the three scenarios, though, is the projection of little impact of grazing on grass production for removal rates of up to 50% of aboveground production. However, prolonged 70% removal rates were counterproductive, resulting in less total consumption by grazers than lighter grazing. Our simulations assume a constant grazing removal rate as a percentage of production, not as a constant amount of biomass removed, as would be expected when a constant herd size is maintained as at WICA. This simplification is reasonable for exploring long-term effects of grazing on production, but it limits our ability to draw conclusions about inter-annual grazing-production interactions in future climate scenarios. High removal in a single year can stimulate forage production, fueled by belowground carbohydrate stores (Loeser et al. 2004), and the heavy levels of grazing on particular sections of the Park may not be deleterious in the short-term, particularly in non-drought years. However, high removal in drought years, due to the lag time in culling herds, will likely have negative consequences.

Our future simulations also projected a consistent decline in the relative production of cool-season (C_3) grasses and a shift to peak grassland production in spring rather than summer. The implications of the former for grazers and their management are difficult to derive. Although one experiment in vegetation similar to that at WICA showed decreased forage quality with increasing CO_2 (Morgan et al. 2004), the complex interactions of temperature, CO_2, and nitrogen that affect forage composition, production, and quality are only beginning to be studied (Morgan et al. 2011). Consequently, their representation in MC1 is somewhat rudimentary. Although forage quality changes are uncertain, changing seasonality of production could have equally important implications for grazer health and reproduction through seasonal forage shortages. Monitoring changes in phenology (perhaps through satellite-determined greenness indices) and forage quality (through clipping and tissue analysis) would improve understanding of the importance of these factors for WICA wildlife.

The presence of bare ground has been found to promote the shift to a high-erosion state in pinyon pine – juniper woodlands (Davenport et al. 1998) and drought-stressed grasses may be slow to recover following heavy grazing. MC1 does not simulate erosion, which is dependent on ground cover, slope and location on the catena (e.g. upper slope vs. valley bottom) (Renard et al. 1991). However, the low summer grass LAI (a measure of grass cover) simulated towards the end of the MIROC future (Figure 16) suggests greater risks of erosion. Soil erosion can reduce productivity, particularly in semi-arid regions, due in part to the formation of surface crusts that increase surface runoff and decrease infiltration, as well as the loss of organic matter and associated nutrients (Vásquez-Méndez et al. 2011). Possible future increases in the intensity of rainfall events (O'Gorman and Schneider 2009) could also decrease infiltration. A rather conservative surface runoff function was used for our WICA simulations, based in part on gauged streamflows for the mostly-forested Beaver Creek watershed (see "Water Balance", above). However, it is likely that some of the substantial geographic variation in forage productivity projected by the empirical forage model of Keller and Millspaugh (2011) reflects spatial variation in infiltration rate. Other non-modeled factors liable to increase spatial variation in forage production include preferential grazing of recently burned areas by bison and the concentration of prairie dog effects in discrete colonies.

These concerns regarding the effects of overgrazing are substantially greater for the Hadley and especially the MIROC futures than for the CSIRO future. Interannual variation in grass cover and productivity are high for the future projections, as well as historically (Figures 15 and 18). There is some increase in inter-year variation in production under all three future climates, which supports the adoption of somewhat more conservative grazing regimes, particularly after 2030. This pattern is of most concern for the MIROC future where ANPP and grass cover drop to quite low levels during the driest years. In contrast, in the CSIRO future, years of high productivity may increase belowground carbohydrate reserves and the capacity of grasses to rebound after dry years.

Conclusions

1. With substantial site-specific adjustments to the parameters and functions affecting grass and tree productivity and fire behavior, we have adapted the dynamic global vegetation model MC1 to simulate the observed ecotone between trees and grasses at Wind Cave National Park.

2. Using this calibration as a base, we projected that the position of the grass – tree ecotone would be little changed for three differing future climate scenarios when prescribed or natural fire regimes are maintained. However, the biomass of wooded areas and the forage production of grasslands may be diminished under hotter and drier scenarios, depending on fire management and grazing intensity.

3. The increases in atmospheric CO_2 that are an important driver of climate change are projected to mitigate the effect of heat and drought on the vegetation, but not entirely so.

4. Increased fire frequencies are simulated for the future, given increased drying of fire fuels. Few crown fires were projected for mature forests because MC1 uses an overall average wind speed (~8 mph). However, simulations with high wind speeds of 30 mph indicate that future fires burning under such conditions will crown, even in mature forests with relatively high crown bases, so long as tree spacing is conducive to carrying such fires. With increased fire frequencies the chance occurrence of fire during such windy weather is increased, and this could produce different forest extent than projected.

5. Currently forested areas may be maintained (at reduced biomass) with prescribed fires, depending on the skill of fire managers in attaining targeted tree mortalities. Results suggest that moderate variation in the timing and intensity of prescribed fires would not severely affect wooded areas, so long as extensive crown fires were avoided. Results also suggest that prescribed fires have the potential to improve or maintain forest health while preventing the incursion of trees into grasslands. Maintaining current or somewhat lower mean basal area over the wooded areas of the park via prescribed burns should make the region more resistant to bark beetle outbreaks than would a fire suppression only approach.

6. Future forage production showed little impact from grazing removal rates up to 50% of aboveground production, but prolonged 70% removal rates resulted in negative impacts to productivity. Future annual forage production varied among climate scenarios, increasing in one and decreasing in another. Mid or late summer declines in productivity due to greater heat and drought occurred in two climate scenarios. This could increase soil erosion in combination with more extreme downpours, as are generally predicted with climate change. Such changes in the seasonality of production could also lead to late-season food shortages for grazers. There is some increase in inter-year variation in production, which supports the adoption of more conservative grazing regimes, particularly after 2030.

7. Given uncertainties in the rate of increase in greenhouse gases and the response of local climate to this forcing, long-term monitoring of production phenology, range quality, species composition, and, in wooded areas, tree density and growth and seedling establishment and survival is of great importance. An important caveat to our results is that MC1 does not yet adequately represent the effects of extreme events on plant communities other than that of fire. Monitoring is also important, given this caveat.

Literature Cited

Allen, C. D., and D. D. Breshears. 1998. Drought-induced shift of a forest-woodland ecotone: rapid landscape response to climate variation. *Proceedings of the National Academy of Sciences, USA* 95:14839-14842.

Allen, C. D., M. Savage, D. A. Falk, K. F. Suckling, T. W. Swetnam, T. Schulke, P. B. Stacey, P. Morgan, M. Hoffman, and J. T. Klingel. 2002. Ecological restoration of Southwestern ponderosa pine ecosystems: a broad perspective. *Ecological Applications* 12:1418-1433.

Anderson, H. E. 1982. Aids to determining fuel models for estimating fire behavior. General Technical Report INT-122. U.S. Forest Service, Ogden, Utah.

Andrews, P. L. 2012. Modeling wind adjustment factor and midflame wind speed for Rothermel's fire spread model. General Technical Report RMRS-266. U.S. Forest Service, Fort Collins, Colorado.

Bachelet, D., J. M. Lenihan, C. Daly, and R. P. Neilson. 2000. Simulated fire, grazing and climate change impacts at Wind Cave National Park, SD. *Ecological Modelling* 134:229–244.

Bachelet, D., J. M. Lenihan, C. Daly, R. P. Neilson, D. S. Ojima, and W. J. Parton. 2001. MC1: A dynamic vegetation model for estimating the distribution of vegetation and associated ecosystem fluxes of carbon, nutrients, and water --technical documentation. Version 1.0. General Technical Report PNW-GTR-508, U.S. Forest Service, Portland, Oregon.

Bachelet D., R. P. Neilson, T. Hickler, R. J. Drapek, J. M. Lenihan, M. T. Sykes, B. Smith, S. Sitch, and K. Thonicke. 2003. Simulating past and future dynamics of natural ecosystems in the United States. *Global Biogeochemical Cycles* 17:1045.

Bader, M. K-F., R. Siegwolf and C. Körner. 2010. Sustained enhancement of photosynthesis in mature deciduous forest trees after 8 years of free air CO_2 enrichment. *Planta* 232:1115-1125.

Baker, W. L. 2009. Fire Ecology in Rocky Mountain Landscapes. Island Press, Washington DC.

Bentz, B. J., J. Règnière, C. J. Fettig, E. M. Hansen, J. L. Hayes, J. A. Hicke, R. G. Kelsey, J. F. Negròn, and S. J. Seybold, S.J. 2010. Climate change and bark beetles of the western United States and Canada: direct and indirect effects. *BioScience* 60:602–613.

Bond, W. J., F. I. Woodward, and G. F. Midgley. 2005. The global distribution of ecosystems in a world without fire. *New Phytologist* 165:525–537.

Bradshaw, L. S., J. E. Deeming, R. E. Burgan and J. D. Cohen 1983. The 1978 national fire danger rating system: a technical documentation. General Technical Report INT-169. U.S. Forest Service, Ogden, Utah.

Brown, P. and C. Sieg. 1999. Historical variability in fire at the ponderosa pine - Northern Great Plains prairie ecotone, southeastern Black Hills, South Dakota. *Ecoscience* 6:539-547.

Brown, P., and B. Cook. 2006. Early settlement forest structure in Black Hills ponderosa pine forests. *Forest Ecology and Management* 223:284-290.

Canham, C. D. 2012. Disentangling responses to climate change versus broad anthropogenic impacts in temperate forests. Ecological Society of America annual meeting abstract.

Cannell, M. G. R. 1982. World Forest Biomass and Primary Production Data. Academic Press, London.

Cogan, D., H. Marriot, J. Von Loh, and M. Pucherelli. 1999. USGS-NPS Vegetation Mapping Program, Wind Cave National Park, South Dakota.

Colorado State Forest Service. 2011. 2011 Report on the Health of Colorado's Forests. Colorado State Forest Service, Fort Collins, Colorado. Available from http://fhm.fs.fed.us/fhh/fhh_11/CO_FHH_2011.pdf.

Daly, C., D. Bachelet, J. M. Lenihan, R. P. Neilson, W. J. Parton, and D. Ojima. 2000. Dynamic simulation of tree-grass interactions for global change studies. *Ecological Applications* 10:449-469.

Davenport, D. W., D. D. Breshears, B. P. Wilcox, and C. D. Allen. 1998. Viewpoint: Sustainability of piñon-juniper ecosystems – a unifying perspective of soil erosion thresholds. *Journal of Range Management* 51:231-240.

DeBlander, L. T. 2002. Forest Resources of the Black Hills National Forest. U.S. Forest Service, Ogden, Utah.

Ehleringer, J. R., and T. E. Cerling. 1995. Atmospheric CO_2 and the ratio of intercellular to ambient CO_2 concentrations in plants. *Tree Physiology* 15:105–111.

Evans, S. E., K. M. Byrne, W. K. Lauenroth, and I. C. Burke. 2011. Defining the limit to resistance in a drought-tolerant grassland: long-term severe drought significantly reduces the dominant species and increases ruderals. *Journal of Ecology* 99:1500-1507.

Fan, Z., X. Fan, M. A. Spetich, S. R. Shifley, W. K. Moser, R. G. Jensen, and J. M. Kabrick. 2011. Developing a stand hazard index for oak decline in upland oak forests of the Ozark Highlands, Missouri. *Northern Journal of Applied Forestry* 28:19-26.

Fan, Z., X. Fan, M. K. Crosby, W. K. Moser, H. He, M. A. Spetich, and S. R. Shifley. 2012. Spatio-temporal trends of oak decline and mortality under periodic regional drought in the Ozark Highlands of Arkansas and Missouri. *Forests* 3:614-631.

Fettig, C.J., Klepzig, K.D., Billings, R.F., Munson, A.S., Nebeker, T.E., Negròn, J.F., Nowak, J.T., 2007. The effectiveness of vegetation management practices for prevention and control of bark beetle infestations in coniferous forests of the western and southern United States. *Forest Ecology and Management* 238:24-53.

Gerhart, L. M., J. M. Harris, J. B. Nippert, D. R. Sandquist and J. K. Ward. 2011. Glacial trees from the La Brea tar pits show physiological constraints of low CO_2. *New Phytologist* 194:63-69.

Gordon, H. B. 2002. The CSIRO Mk3 climate system model. CSIRO Atmospheric Research Technical Paper 60. CSIRO, Aspendale, Victoria, Australia.

Gordon, W. S., J. S. Famiglietti, N. L. Fowler, T. G. F. Kittel and K. A. Hibbard. 2004. Validation of simulated runoff from six terrestrial ecosystem models: Results from VEMAP. *Ecological Applications* 14:527-545.

Graham, R. T., A. E. Harvey, T. B. Jain, and J. R. Tonn. 1999. The effects of thinning and similar stand treatments on fire behavior in western forests. General Technical Report PNW-GTR-463. U.S. Forest Service, Portland, Oregon.

Halbert, N., P. J. P. Gogan, R. Hiebert, and J. N. Derr. 2007. Where the buffalo roam: The role of history and genetics in the conservation of bison on U.S. federal lands. *Park Science* 24:22-29.

Hasumi, H., and S. Emori, editors. 2004. K-1 coupled GCM (MIROC) description. K-1 Technical Report 1. Center for Climate System Research, Tokyo, Japan. Available at http://www.ccsr.utokyo.ac.jp/kyosei/hasumi/MIROC/tech-repo.pdf.

Holecheck, J. L., H. Gomez, F. Molinar and D. Galt. 1999. Grazing studies: What we've learned. *Rangelands* 21:12-16.

Hood, S., S. Smith, D. Cluck, E. Reinhardt and K. Ryan. 2008. Delayed tree mortality following fire in western conifers. JFSP # 05-2-1-105 Final Report. Available from http://www.firescience.gov/projects/05-2-1-105/project/05-2-1-105_05-2-1-105_final_report.pdf.

Hostetler, S. W., J. R. Adler, and A. M. Allan. 2011. Dynamically downscaled climate simulations over North America: Methods, evaluation and supporting documentation for users. Open File Report 2011-1238. U.S. Geological Survey, Reston, Virginia.

IPCC. 2007. Climate change 2007: the physical science basis. Contribuiton of Working Group I to the Fourth Assessment Report of the Intergovernmental Panel on Climate Change [S. Solomon, D. Qin, M. Manning, Z. Chen, M.Marquis, K.B. Averyt, M. Tignor, and H.L. Miller (editors)]. Cambridge University Press, Cambridge, United Kingdom.

Iversen, C. M. 2010. Digging deeper: fine-root responses to rising atmospheric CO_2 concentration in forested ecosystems. *New Phytologist* 186:346-357.

Jackson, R. B., C. W. Cook, J. S. Pippen, and S. M. Palmer. 2009. Increased belowground biomass and soil CO_2 fluxes after a decade of carbon dioxide enrichment in a warm-temperate forest. *Ecology* 90:3352-3366.

Johns, T. C., J. M. Gregory, W. J. Ingram, C. E. Johnson, A. Jones, J. A. Lowe, J. F. B. Mitchell, D. L. Roberts, D. M. H. Sexton, D. S. Stevenson, S. F. B. Tett, M. J. Woodage. 2003. Anthropogenic climate change for 1860 to 2100 simulated with the HadCM3 model under updated emissions scenarios, *Climate Dynamics* 20:583–612.

Joyce, L. A., D. E. Chalk, and A. Vigil. 1986. Range forage data base for 20 Great Plains, Southern, and Western states. General Technical Report RM-133. U.S. Forest Service, Fort Collins, Colorado.

Keller, B. J., and J. J. Millspaugh. 2010. Forage production and allocation model for Wind Cave National Park: Project Report PMIS 112661, Number BR-07-15. University of Missouri Unpublished Report, Columbia, Missouri.

Kercher, J.R. and M. C. Axelrod. 1984. A process model of fire ecology and succession in a mixed-conifer forest. *Ecology*. 65:1725-1742.

Kern, J. S. 1995. Geographic patterns of soils water-holding capacity in the contiguous United States. *Soil Science Society of America* 59:1126-1133.

Kern, J. S. 2000. Erratum for Geographic patterns of soils water-holding capacity in the contiguous United States. *Soil Science Society of America* 64:382-382.

King, D. A. 2011. Size-related changes in tree proportions and their potential influence on the course of height growth. Pages 165-191 *in* F. C. Meinzer, B. Lachenbruch, and T. E. Dawson, editors. Size- and age-related changes in tree structure and function. Springer, Dordrecht.

King, D. A., D. P. Turner and W. D. Ritts. 2011. Parameterization of a diagnostic carbon cycle model for continental scale application. *Remote Sensing of Environment* 115:1653-1664.

Kolb, P. K., and R. Robberecht. 1996. High temperature and drought stress effects on the survival of *Pinus ponderosa* seedlings. *Tree Physiology* 16:665-672.

Körner, C., R. Asshoff, O. Bignucolo, S. Hättenschwiler, S. G. Keel, S. Pelaez-Riedl, S. Pepin R. T. W. Siegwolf and G. Zotz. 2005. Carbon flux and growth in mature deciduous forest trees exposed to elevated CO_2. *Science* 309:1360–1362

Lee, T. D, S. H. Barrott, and P. H. Reich 2011. Photosynthetic responses of 13 grassland species across 11 years of free air CO_2 enrichment is modest, consistent and independent of N supply. *Global Change Biology* 17:2893-2904.

Lenihan, J. M., C. Daly, D. Bachelet, and R. P. Neilson 1998. Simulating broad-scale fire severity in a dynamic global vegetation model. *Northwest Science* 72:91–101.

Lenihan, J. M., R. J. Drapek, D. Bachelet, and R. P. Neilson. 2003. Climate changes effects on vegetation distribution, carbon, and fire in California. *Ecological Applications* 13:1667-1681.

Lenihan, J. M., D. Bachelet, R. P. Neilson, and R. Drapek. 2008. Simulated response of conterminous United States ecosystems to climate change at different levels of fire suppression, CO_2 emission rate, and growth response to CO_2. *Global and Planetary Change* 64:16-25.

Le Quéré, C., M. R. Raupach, J. G. Canadell, G. Marland, L. Bopp, P. Ciais, T. J. Conway, S. C. Doney, R. A. Feely, P. Foster, P. Friedlingstein, K. Gurney, R. A. Houghton, J. I. House, C. Huntingford, P. E. Levy, M. R. Lomas, J. Majkut, N. Metzl, J. P. Ometto, G. P. Peters, I. C. Prentice, J. T. Randerson, S. W. Running, J. L. Sarmiento, U. Schuster, S. Sitch, T. Takahashi, N. Viovy, G. R. van der Werf, and F. I. Woodward. 2009. Trends in the sources and sinks of carbon dioxide. *Nature Geoscience* 2:831-836.

Li, J.-H., P. Dijkstra, C. R. Hinkle, R. M. Wheeler, and B. G. Drake. 1999. Photosynthetic acclimation to elevated atmospheric CO_2 concentration in the Florida scrub-oak species *Quercus geminata* and *Quercus myrtifolia* growing in their native environment. *Tree Physiology* 19:229-234.

Lindsay, A. A., J. D. Barton Jr., and S. R. Miles. 1958. Field efficiencies of forest sampling methods. *Ecology* 39:428-444.

Loeser, M. R., T. E. Crews, and T. D. Sisk. 2004. Defoliation increased above-ground productivity in a semi-arid grassland. *Rangeland Ecology and Management* 57:442-447.

Litschert, S. E., T. C. Brown, and D. M. Theobald. 2012. Historic and future extent of wildfires in the Southern Rockies Ecoregion, USA. *Forest Ecology and Management* 269:124-133.

Maraun, D., F. Wetterhall, A. M. Ireson, R. E. Chandler, E. J. Kendon, M. Widmann, S. Brienen, H. W. Rust, T. Sauter, M. ThemeBl, V. K. C. Venema, K. P. Chun, C. M. Goodess, R. G. Jones, C. Onof, M. Vrac and I. Thiele-Eich. 2010. Precipitation downscaling under climate change: Recent developments to bridge the gap between dynamical models and the end user. *Reviews of Geophysics* 48:RG3003.

Marriot, H., D. Faber-Langendoen, A. McAdams, D. Stutzman, and B. Burkhart. 1999. Black Hills Community Inventory, Final Report. The Nature Conservancy, Minneapolis, Minnesota.

McCarthy H. R., R. Oren A, Finzi, and K. H. Johnsen. 2006. Canopy leaf area constrains [CO_2]-induced enhancement of productivity and partitioning among aboveground carbon pools. *Proceedings of the National Academy of Sciences, USA* 103: 19356–19361.

Metherell, A. K., L. A. Harding, C. V. Cole and W. J. Parton. 1993. CENTURY soil organic matter model environment: Technical Documentation. Agroecosystem Version 4.0. Great Plains System Research Unit Technical Report No. 4. Agricultural Research Service, Fort Collins, Colorado.

Milchunas, D. G., and W. K. Lauenroth. 1993. Quantitative effects of grazing on vegetation and soils over a global range of environments. *Ecological Monographs* 63:327-366.

Morgan, J. A., A. R. Mosier, D. G. Milchunas, D. R. LeCain, J. A. Nelson, and W. J. Parton. 2004. CO_2 enhances productivity of the shortgrass steppe, alters species composition, and reduces forage digestibility. *Ecological Applications* 14:208-219.

Morgan, J. A., D. R. LeCain, E. Pendall, D. M. Blumenthal, B. A. Kimball, Y. Carrillo, D. G. Williams, J. Heisler-White, F. A. Dijkstra, and M. West. 2011. C_4 grasses prosper as carbon dioxide eliminates desiccation in warmed semi-arid grassland. *Nature* 476:202-206.

Myers, C. A., and J. L. Van Deusen. 1960. Site index of ponderosa pine in the Black Hills from soil and topography. *Journal of Forestry* 58:548-551, 554-555.

Niinemets, U., and F. Valladares. 2006. Tolerance to shade, drought, and waterlogging of temperate northern hemisphere trees and shrubs. *Ecological Monographs* 76:521-547.

Negròn, J.F., McMillin, J.D., Anhold, J.A., Coulson, D., 2009. Bark beetle-caused mortality in a drought-affected ponderosa pine landscape in Arizona, USA. *Forest Ecology and Management* 257:1353–1362.

Nakićenović, N., J. Alcamo, G. Davis, B. de Vries, J. Fenhann, S. Gaffin, K. Gregory, A. Grübler, T. Y. Jung, T. Kram, and others. 2000. Emissions Scenarios: A Special Report of Working Group III of the Intergovernmental Panel on Climate Change. Cambridge University Press, Cambridge, United Kingdom.

Norby R. J., E. H. DeLucia, B. Gielen, C. Calfapietra, C. P. Giardina, J. S. King, J. Ledford, H. R. McCarthy, D. J. P. Moore, R. Ceulemans, and others. 2005. Forest response to elevated CO_2 is conserved across a broad range of productivity. *Proceedings of the National Academy of Sciences, USA* 102: 18052–18056.

Norby R. J., J. M. Warren, C. M. Iversen, B. E. Medlyn and R. E. McMurtrie. 2010. CO_2 enhancement of forest productivity constrained by limited nitrogen availability. *Proceedings of the National Academy of Sciences, USA* 107:19368–73

Norby, R. J., and D. R. Zak. 2011. Ecological lessons from free-air CO_2 enrichment (FACE) experiments. *Annual Reviews of Ecology and Systematics* 42:181-203.

Nösberger J., S. P. Long, R. J. Norby, M. Stitt, G. R. Hendrey, and H. Blum, edirors. 2006. Managed ecosystems and CO_2. Springer-Verlag, Berlin, Germany.

Nowacki, G. J., and M. D. Abrams. 2008. The demise of fire and 'mesophication' of forests in the eastern United States. *Bioscience* 58:123-138.

O'Gorman, P. A. and T. Schneider. 2009. The physical basis for increases in precipitation extremes in simulations of 21st-century climate change. *Proceedings of the National Academy of Sciences, USA* 106:14773-14777.

Oliver, W. W., and R. A. Ryker. 1990. *Pinus ponderosa* Dougl. ex Laws. Ponderosa pine. Pages 173-180 *in* Burns, R. M., and R. H. Honkola, editors. Silvics of North America. Agriculture Handbook 654. U.S. Forest Service, Washington, DC.

Oliver, C. D., and B. C. Larson. 1996. Forest Stand Dynamics. John Wiley & Sons Inc., New York, New York.

Parton, W. J. 1984. Predicting soil temperatures in a shortgrass steppe. *Soil Science* 138:93-101.

Peterson, D. L., and K. C. Ryan. 1986. Modeling postfire conifer mortality for long-range planning. *Environmental Management* 10:797-808.

Rehfeldt, G. E., N. L. Crookston, M. V. Warwell, and J. S. Evans. 2006. Empirical analyses of plant-climate relationships for the western United States. *International Journal of Plant Science* 167:1123–1150.

Reinhardt, E. D., and N. L. Crookston, Technical Editors. 2003. The Fire and Fuels Extension to the Forest Vegetation Simulator. General Technical Report RMRS-GTR-116. U.S. Forest Service, Ogden, Utah.

Rejmánek, M. and M. J. Pitcairn. 2002. When is eradication of exotic pest plants a realistic goal? Pages 249–253 *in* C. R. Veitch and M. N. Clout, editors. Turning the Tide: The Eradication of Invasive Species. Invasive Species Specialist Group of the World Conservation Union, Auckland, New Zealand.

Renard, K. G., G. R. Foster, G. A. Weesies, and J. P. Porter. 1991. RUSLE: Revised universal soil loss equation. *Journal of Soil and Water Conservation* 46:30-33.

Ripple, W. J. and R. L. Beschta, R.L., 2007. Hardwood tree decline following the loss of large carnivores on the Great Plains, USA. *Frontiers in Ecology and the Environment* 5:241–246.

Rogers, B. M., R. P. Neilson, R. Drapek, J. M. Lenihan, J. R. Wells, D. Bachelet, and B. E. Law. 2011. Impacts of climate change on fire regimes and carbon stocks of the U.S. Pacific Northwest. *Journal of Geophysical Research* 116:G03037.

Rothermel, R. 1972. A mathematical model for fire spread predictions in wildland fuels. Research Paper INT-RP-115. U.S. Forest Service, Ogden, Utah.

Ryan, K. C. and E. D. Reinhardt. 1988. Predicting postfire mortality of seven western conifers. *Canadian Journal of Forest Research* 18:1291-1297.

Sala, O. E., W. J. Parton, L. A. Joyce and W. K. Lauenroth. 1988. Primary production of the central grassland region of the United-States. *Ecology* 69:40-45.

Schmid, J. M., S. A. Mata, W. K. Olsen, and D. D. Vigil. 1993. Phloem temperatures in mountain pine beetle-infested ponderosa pine. Research Note RM-521. U.S. Forest Service, Fort Collins, Colorado.

Shafer, S. L., P. J. Bartlein and R. S. Thompson. 2001. Potential changes in the distributions of western North America tree and shrub taxa under future climate scenarios. *Ecosystems* 4:200-215.

Sillett S. C., R. Van Pelt, G. W. Cook, A. R. Ambrose, A. L. Carroll, M. E. Antoine, and B. M. Mifsud. 2010. Increasing wood production through old age in tall trees. *Forest Ecology and Management* 259:976-994.

Soulé, P. T. and P. A. Knapp. 2006. Radial growth rate increases in naturally occurring ponderosa pine trees: a late-20th century CO_2 fertilization effect? *New Phytologist* 171:379-390.

Symstad, A. J. and M. Bynum. 2005. The extent and significance of old-growth ponderosa pine forest at Mount Rushmore National Memorial. U.S. Geological Survey Unpublished Report, Keystone, South Dakota.

USDA Natural Resources Conservation Service. 1990. Soil Survey of Custer and Pennington Counties, Black Hills Parts, South Dakota. National Cooperative Soil Survey

USDA Natural Resources Conservation Service. 1996. Soil Survey of Custer and Pennington Counties, Prairie Parts, South Dakota. National Cooperative Soil Survey.

Van Haverbeke, D. F. Genetic variation in ponderosa pine: a 15-year test of provenances in the Great Plains. 1986. Research Paper RM-265. U.S. Forest Service, Fort Collins, Colorado.

Van Wagner, C. E. 1993. Prediction of crown fire behavior in 2 stands of jack pine. *Canadian Journal of Forest Research* 23:442–449.

Van Wagner, C.E., and Pickett, T.L. 1985. Equations and FORTRAN program for the Canadian Forest Fire Weather Index System. Canadian Forest Service Forest Technical Report 33. Canadian Forestry Service, Petawawa National Forestry Institute, Chalk River, Ontario.

Vásquez-Méndez, R., E. Ventura-Ramos, K. Oleschko, L. Hernández-Sandoval, and M. A. Domínguez-Cortázar. 2011. Soil erosion processes in semiarid areas: The importance of native vegetation. Pages 25-40 *in* D. Godone, editor. Soil Erosion Studies, ISBN: 978-953-307-710-9, InTech, Available from: http://www.intechopen.com/books/soil-erosion-studies/soil-erosion-processes-in-semiarid-areas-the-importance-of-native-vegetation.

Warren J. M., E. Pötzelsberger, S. D. Wullschleger, H. Hasenauer, P. E. Thornton, and R. J. Norby. 2011. Ecohydrological impact of reduced stomatal conductance in forests exposed to elevated CO_2. *Ecohydrology* 4:196-210

WeatherDisc Associates. 1995. World WeatherDisc: climate data for planet Earth. WeatherDisc Associates, Seattle, Washington.

Weller, D. E. 1989. The interspecific size-density relationship among crowded plant stands and its implications for the -3/2 power rule of self-thinning. *American Naturalist* 133:20-41.

Westerling, A. L., M. G. Turner, E. A. H. Smithwick, W. H. Romme, and M. G. Ryan. 2011. Continued warming could transform Greater Yellowstone fire regimes by mid-21st century. *Proceedings of the National Academy of Sciences, USA* 108:13165–13170.

Wind Cave National Park Division of Resource Management. 2009. Forage Management Wind Cave National Park 2001-2009. National Park Service Unpublished, Draft Report, Hot Springs, South Dakota.

Wyckoff, P. H. and R. Bowers. 2010. Response of the prairie-forest border to climate change: impacts of increasing drought may be mitigated by increasing CO_2. *Journal of Ecology* 98:197-208.

Zausen, G. L., T. E. Kolb, J. D. Bailey, and M. R. Wagner. 2005. Long-term impacts of stand management on ponderosa pine physiology and bark beetle abundance in northern Arizona: a replicated landscape study. *Forest Ecology and Management* 218:291–305.

NPS 108/119713, January 2013